The
Health Advocate's
Advanced
Marketing Handbook

by
Trisha Torrey,
Every Patient's Advocate

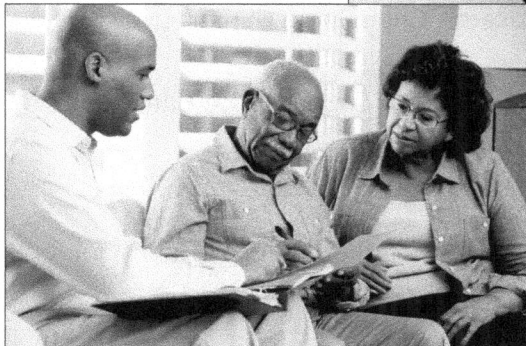

The Health Advocate's Advanced Marketing Handbook

Copyright @2014   by Trisha Torrey, Every Patient's Advocate All Rights Reserved.

ISBN: 978-0-9828014-4-4

HealthAdvocateResources.com

Trisha Torrey, Every Patient's Advocate
1-888-478-6588
contact@diagKNOWsis.com

Discounts for bulk-orders of this book are available by contacting the author. Trisha Torrey is also available for speaking opportunities to groups of patients or professionals.

diagKNOWsis™   DiagKNOWsis Media
                      PO Box 53
                      Baldwinsville, NY 13027
                      www.DiagKNOWsis.com

Also from DiagKNOWsis Media:

♦ You Bet Your Life! The 10 Mistakes Every Patient Makes
  (How to Fix Them to Get the Healthcare You Deserve)

This book is #4 in the series for Health and Patient Advocates.
Also available:

1. So You Want to Be a Patient Advocate? Choosing a Career
    in Health or Patient Advocacy

2. The Health Advocate's Start and Grow Your Own Practice Handbook

3. The Health Advocate's Basic Marketing Handbook

4. This book

5. The Health Advocate's Low and No Cost Marketing Ideas Handbook
    (available in 2015)

Printed in the United States of America
CS15

Dedication

Health Advocacy as a profession has grown
exponentially since it began to get legs in 2009.
Thousands of patients have benefited from the
efforts of this growing group of dedicated pioneers
who work tirelessly on their behalf.

So, as I did for the first two books in this series,
I dedicate this book to "my" advocates—members
of the Alliance of Professional Health Advocates —
who have devoted themselves to helping others get
the best from the healthcare system.

Thanks to you all, from
the bottom of
my heart.

Trisha Torrey

Yes, "Advanced"

I expect there will be some folks who will consider simply skipping the first marketing book, *The Health Advocate's Basic Marketing Handbook,* in favor of this more advanced book, thinking you'll save yourself some time and money.

If you do so, and unless you have handled marketing for a small business in the past (and yes, I know there are some of you who have!), then you may have difficulty making your way through this book.

No "basics" are included in this advanced book. Where the basics are required, I've made notations to that effect. But I haven't reiterated them because they've already been written and explained in the Basic book. There was no sense in writing them again, then asking you to pay for them twice.

As it says on page 11, the Basic book* teaches you how to do the marketing walk. This Advanced book teaches you how to do the marketing dance.

You'll have trouble learning to dance if you haven't learned to walk first.

Trisha Torrey
Author
The Health Advocate's
Advanced Marketing Handbook

The Health Advocate's Basic Marketing Handbook

Table of Contents

...more on next page...

Table of Contents, continued...

Introduction

H ealth and patient advocacy as a profession is growing fast in a very unusual, sort of leapfrog fashion, differently from most professions.

Like this:

Patients and their caregivers need help but may not know that the type of help they need even exists. They may be aware that there is someone in the hospital who can help. They may think to ask at their doctor's office. Often they voice their frustrations to others – friends or family or even someone at church. Eventually they may do a search online, but without knowing to look for "patient advocate" or "navigator" – they just have to keep looking until they finally stumble across the concept of a private, independent advocate. Once they find us, they experience relief, and a sort-of "aha!" moment.

Then there are advocates; people with interest and the skills to help patients, offering to help, sometimes in a sort of ad hoc fashion, because a friend or loved one needs help. Maybe they have a background in medicine, maybe not. Maybe they have dreamed about doing this work as a career, but the response to the call for help compels them to consider it seriously. They already know they have advocacy skills, but actually running a business – well that's another story.

The problem is that patients and advocates aren't necessarily doing those things at the same time. Patients just know they need help, not realizing there is a profession that has been built to help them. Advocates offer services that patients haven't identified as a need yet and get frustrated because no one is hiring them. Too often patients and advocates are like star-crossed lovers, looking in the wrong places, or at the wrong times, understanding the need and work differently, yet still, desperately, wanting and needing each other.

Business, and the Concept of Star-Crossed Lovers

There was one other time in my life when I experienced this sort of phenomenon.

In the mid-1990s I began to realize what the World Wide Web could become. At the time I was the marketing director for my local community college. Our main target audience was, of course, young adults who were within a few years of high school and didn't want to go out of town to college. They were beginning to "surf" the Internet – a new term in those days!

There were very few businesses or organizations, much less colleges, that offered information on the web then. So I took classes to learn HTML (the computer language that is the basis for most websites, even today.) Then, evenings and weekends, I built a very rudimentary website for my community college. I put everything there that would look enticing – smiling faces, books and classrooms…. I used some of the material we had already printed in our catalogue and in brochures and simply repurposed it for the website.

It was new! And cool! And we got lots of press about it because it was so different. Those young adults loved it. Enrollments begin to climb. We had figured out a new way to reach the right audience, with the right message, through the right medium – just the basics of marketing – and it worked.

So what similarity does that have to marketing advocacy? Well, that's what came next.

The press the college received was enough to compel a large, local marketing agency to contact me, and to make me an offer I could not refuse. Just a few months into my tenure with the agency, I proposed creation of a new web development service that the agency could offer to its clients. Knowing that marketing on the web would be the NEXT BIG THING, the principles at the agency jumped at it, gave me a new title, all the resources I could need – and voila! With great excitement, two of us started up a new web development department. In early 1999 we began to roll it out to our clients and….

Thud.

No interest. Not one client took a bite of our great offer to build them a new marketing-focused website. It was quickly very clear why they weren't interested. **It was because they didn't think their target audiences were online**. Knowing the key to effective marketing is to identify your target audiences, then to find them, and put the information they need in front of them – they didn't think it made sense for them to spend the money for a website. (Heck, even in the late 1990s, some of them were still trying to decide whether to begin using computers in their offices.)

So there we were – star-crossed lovers. The agency was offering a service we knew they needed. They weren't sure what they needed and didn't yet see the value we could bring….

So my job shifted a bit. It was no longer about offering a service to our lowest hanging fruit – our current clients. The new approach was to find businesses that already recognized the value of being online, because they knew well that their potential customers already WERE online.

So – channeling Crosby, Stills and Nash… *If you can't be with the one you love, then love the one you're with!* We found new clients who wanted and needed us, and went to work for them.

Then - from thud to rocket launch... In less than 12 months we had 13 people in our department and just could not keep up with the workload. All of a sudden, every client who had dismissed our web development offer just a few months earlier, plus many more, realized their customers had caught the surfing wave, and they wanted a piece of it in the form of a new website – yesterday. We had been on to something after all, and the business grew.[1]

Subtracting the "Crossed" from the Stars

I could draw a dozen more parallels between the discovery of the benefits to businesses and their customers of using the Internet and the World Wide Web - to the benefits to the healthcare system of patients and providers embracing advocacy. But the key point is that it didn't take long for the marketplace of businesses and potential customers to shift from not really recognizing those benefits to a point where it not only recognized them, but – in true new lover fashion – they just couldn't get enough of each other.

No longer were they star-crossed at all. That's where we think advocacy is headed too.

Now, I take no credit whatsoever for the growth of the use of the web for marketing and information! That's not the point. Instead, the point is that I recognized the web for the tool it could become, and then I just applied standard, good, smart marketing practice to help the agency I worked for grow that part of its business.

And that's what I try to teach advocates. That if we use good, basic marketing, including finding the right target audiences, developing, then reaching them with smart messages, at the right time, using the right tools, then we'll launch our rockets too.

What You Will Find in This Book

The assumptions I've made (yes, I know what they say about assumptions!) while writing this book are that you have had some success in the early stages of your health advocacy practice, that you've worked out some of the kinks that go with the territory in any new business, and that you are ready to work on growing your practice and your personal brand in parallel, because each depends on the other's success.

I've written this book as if it is being read and embraced by the decision-maker for a small practice, say a solo practitioner up to four or five people, maybe employees, or maybe independent contractors, who work together to provide services to clients.

No doubt the advice can be used by larger practices as well. In a large practice, the marketing and business growth decision-makers can use this information in more targeted ways within subgroups of their enterprises.

---

1   A sidenote if you are interested: I lasted at the agency for about two more years before I was so totally burned out that I knew I needed to make a change. I left to start my own marketing business in late 2001, mostly moving small businesses to the web, when I had my (now legendary!) run-in with the healthcare system in 2004. (http://everypatientsadvocate.com/misdiagnosis.htm) That, of course, is what compelled me to shift my work to patient empowerment and advocacy.

I'm also going to assume (despite what "they" say!) that your intent is to grow your business through marketing.[2]

- you are looking for more clients
- you hope to make more money from the clients you already work with
- you need to replace the clients who go away (maybe you solve their problem, or maybe they die, or anything in between.)

This book should be a match that, once struck, will spark some new, creative ideas to help make any and all of those goals happen. It is full of new ways of looking at your world to find new opportunities for your business.

Implementation of these new ideas should take you from owning not only your own practice, but to owning your own higher profile too. You'll take a great deal of pride in what you can accomplish, and your ability to share your expertise in a variety of ways that aren't just about attracting one new client at a time.

What This Book Isn't

The concepts in this book are not intended to be a quick fix to a lagging practice. If your practice doesn't have a strong foundation to begin with, then employing advanced marketing tactics will not likely turn it around.

Further, there is no attempt in this book to be "low and no cost". If it is relevant, I'll discuss cost as we go along. You'll find most of the ideas require time, but not money. Time is, of course, its own expense.

Finally, those who have used the first two books in this series (*The Health Advocate's Start and Grow Your Own Practice Handbook* and *The Health Advocate's Basic Marketing Handbook*) and have used the downloadable workbooks, may be surprised to see that there is no similar workbook for this book. That's because it's not necessary. We aren't building a marketing strategy or a marketing or business plan – your plans should have been completed with those books, although you would be wise to go back and update them based on the new strategies in this book.

(You will find some exercises included to help you make your own notes as you go along so you can kick start your own implementation.)

How to Use This Advanced Marketing Handbook

In *The Health Advocate's Basic Marketing Handbook*, we took a thorough look at marketing basics – how to think them through, how to create a strategy and how to execute that strategy using some beginning tactics. The basic book was Marketing for Advocates 101.

---

2   There are many more ways to grow a business – adding products and services, hiring new people with new capabilities, setting up a second location, or others. This book will focus on the acquisition of new clients, retention of current clients, and sales of additional services to the clients you are already working with.

Those basics are very much the foundation for this book, *The Health Advocate's Advanced Marketing Handbook.* In this book we will tackle the next steps, some advanced strategies, like finding additional audiences that may not be obvious at first, but may be even easier to find success with; adjusting our messaging to make it even more effective for those new audiences, establishing a recognized expertise, using the web in some more effective ways – in general, and overall expansion of and efficient use of those basics.

This advanced book is Marketing 201 and beyond.

Whereas the *Basic Marketing Handbook* uses a linear, step-by-step, put one foot in front of the other to build a basic marketing strategy, this book is not that at all.

This advanced book will capitalize on the basics to help you use them in more powerful, sometimes very unique ways. These advanced strategies and tactics are of the pick-and-choose variety. You don't have to try them all, and you probably won't need all of them. Each of them will rely on the basics, and you'll use them to expand and extend your business and your brand.

▲

Strategies vs. Tactics

As a review to help you get your arms around all this:

A strategy is a plan of action that will help you achieve your goals. For example, one strategy is to create more awareness of your brand so it will become recognizable. Another strategy will be to create a niche so that you can focus your marketing until your clients fit into that niche.

A tactic is the way you execute that strategy – how you make it happen. For example, to create more awareness of your brand, you will include your logo and positioning statement (tag line) on your brochures, your websites, your blog, and on all the slides you make for your PowerPoint presentations. Another tactic might be to run an ad in your community newspaper that includes both your logo and tag line.

▼

The Basic book taught you to do the marketing walk. This book teaches you how to do the marketing dance.

(Alternatively, if you don't understand the basics, and you aren't already employing them in your practice's marketing, then this book will be a real challenge for you. Just as you would have trouble dancing if you couldn't walk, you'll have trouble understanding this advanced book if you don't already employ the basics. I suggest you go back to the *Basic Marketing Handbook*, reread, and implement the ideas that are there – then return to try these ideas.)

I've divided the book into three sections:

• **The first section is about assessing where your marketing is today**. You'll learn how to do a SWOT Analysis: Strengths, Weaknesses, Opportunities and Threats. With that analysis in hand, you'll have a better idea of what's working, and what isn't, in your advocacy marketing environment.

• **The second section addresses advanced strategies**. Beyond the basic strategies outlined in *The Health*

Advocate's Basic Marketing Handbook, these will help you expand your brand, develop your marketing niche, become a recognized expert, and then extend your reach with some new target audiences.

- Making your strategies work requires smart tactics, so that's what we'll address in the third section. We did a solid review of basic tactics, like advertising and public relations, in the Basic Marketing Handbook. So now we'll expand on those, with a thorough look at public speaking, customer service and web tactics galore.

To make the most from this book, you'll want to use Chapter One, Your Marketing SWOT Analysis, to determine what old strategies need to be adjusted, and then determine which new strategies outlined in this advanced book can expand your reach.

Then you can apply the tactics from both books to those newly revised and updated strategies.

A Bonus for You—the ORB

Resources and references change so frequently that I've decided to include them, with live links, online. To that end, I have built

The ORB – the Advocate's Online Resource Bank.

You'll see this logo (ORB) **which shows you that resources for that section**
have been added to the site at:
www.HealthAdvocateResources.com/ORB

You'll find references to the ORB throughout the book. It will stay updated with new resources, or updates to the links for current resources. This will serve you far better than making you type out all those long web addresses.

So let's get started, first with a quick review of your current marketing to figure out what holes we need to fill. Then using that review, we'll determine what the opportunities are for growing your business through some new marketing ideas.

Chapter One

What's Working, and What Isn't? Your Marketing SWOT Analysis

Since you've probably been in practice for a little while now, you know that there is little time to stop and think about what works and what doesn't. You're so busy trying to just DO BUSINESS, and CARE FOR CLIENTS! Who has time to learn new things, stay current with healthcare related news, make sure you're being paid the money you've earned and not paying out more than is absolutely necessary, plus juggling family, home responsibilities, your social life and an occasional hour of sleep?

This is where I remind you that working hard isn't the same as working smart.

Working smart means you are moving that needle on making more and more of your hours billable (as opposed to non-billable administrative hours), accomplishing the many tasks you perform in their most efficient and effective ways, and finding the balance you need in your life. That's how you maximize your business income while minimizing your business headaches.

Working hard, on the other hand, is what most of us do until some, usually external force (like an advanced marketing book) slaps us upside the head to remind us that maybe we aren't being as efficient and effective as we could be, and that possibly taking a few hours to assess that will save us many hours, and money, in the long run. That sort of exercise can minimize the headaches, and open the door to maximizing income.

Now, I'm not going to make you undertake a review of your entire business structure or work product here. But I am going to help you make an assessment of the marketing portion of your work to be sure the decisions you make going forward are focused on the gaps that need to be filled. Doing so will make your marketing smarter, and therefore work harder for you - allowing you to just be smart.

A Marketing SWOT Analysis

SWOT = Strengths, Weaknesses, Opportunities and Threats

A SWOT analysis is an audit, an inventory, a snapshot of sorts, which sets the stage for your next round of business focus. SWOT analyses take place at every level of a business. You may have participated in such an exercise in a previous job and if so, you have a sense of how it can help you capitalize on what's working, and clean up what isn't.

For our purposes, we're going to do a Marketing SWOT analysis. We're going to examine your current marketing, and the environment in which you are working. This exercise will help you figure out what does work and what isn't working as well as it should (or as well as you would like). Included are outside forces that affect your work, and therefore your marketing. In the end, it will reveal the gaps that exist in your marketing that need to be filled.

The goal of this book is to help you fill those gaps and then go a few steps further.[3]

SWOTs actually represent two realms of your work:

Strengths and Weaknesses are internal – they relate directly to your work, how you perform your work, the results of your work, and the consequences (positive and negative) of your own decision making. Strengths are those abilities you have and things you do that add value to your marketing. Weaknesses are the things you do, and the abilities, or lack thereof, that stand in the way of your good marketing, and therefore put you at a competitive disadvantage.

Find a Marketing Buddy

This SWOT analysis is a great exercise to do with someone else because two heads are always better than one.

So why not find someone else to collaborate with? As the advocacy profession grows, there are dozens or hundreds of others, just like you, who are establishing small practices, just like you, who could benefit from such an alliance.

When you attend advocacy gatherings (conferences, workshops), or if you are taking advocacy courses, you may meet others with similar interests. You may also find them online in discussion forums, for example. (Why not request one in the Alliance of Professional Health Advocates Forum?) Connect with someone you think you'd like to work with and ask them if they would like to work with you to support each other's SWOT analyses.

Your best bet is to find someone who works in a different geography from yours so you can freely share ideas, and test out each other's ideas, without stepping on toes.

Once you've worked on the SWOT analyses together, you can remain supportive business-building buddies for any number of additional aspects of your work.

---

3   Let me note here that this overview is intended to help you do a SWOT analysis of your marketing only. You could undertake a SWOT analysis of your entire business if you think it's helpful (it is). Find SWOT information and resources in the Online Resource Bank—the ORB.

Opportunities and Threats are external – they relate to those forces outside of your control, both positive and negative, that affect how you do your work, and your marketing. They describe your marketplace, such as the people you are trying to influence, your geography, the services you offer (or don't offer), even the ability of your potential audiences to pay for your services. You cannot control opportunities and threats. You can only control your own response to them.

That's really all the background you need to get started. It will make far more sense once you jump in to figure it out. So now – let's do your Marketing SWOT analysis.

▲

EXERCISE—Marketing SWOT Analysis

Set up two sheets of paper (or the electronic equivalent) and write one of these words at the top of each:

STRENGTHS   WEAKNESSES

(Stick today's date on there too. You might want to revisit them in the future to see what kinds of progress you have made.)

Remember, your lists of strengths and weaknesses are about those things you actually have control over. No matter whether you perceive a list item as a strength or as a weakness – you could change its designation if you try to because you are the person who has domain over it.

An example of a strength you might have would be that your clients always submit a testimonial on your behalf when you complete your work with them – or (put another way) that you have a knack for twisting their arms to do so. Another example is that you have made your way into the hearts and minds of local providers who realize your value and happily recommend you to their patients. Being listed in the AdvoConnection Directory is definitely a strength. Another example of a strength is that you've successfully made it on-to the local speaking circuit and that you're able to address a different group once a month or three or four times a year.

An example of a marketing weakness might be that you can't seem to nail the best times or places to advertise. You've run ads in your local community paper, or even used Google ads a few times, but the phone hasn't yet rung. Another might be that you've haven't succeeded in getting local press to feature your work in some way, even though you've tried to make that connection. Another might be that you just don't feel confident about the marketing you do, or the admission that you just don't like marketing. (If you use that one, just be sure you aren't confusing marketing with sales.[4] Most people, once they

---

4   Marketing supports sales. In large corporations they are two different departments. Marketing is about strategy, tactics, messages and media. When marketing is done well and right, it means that making sales is far easier. Sales means asking someone to sign a contract, then pay for the work or product. Find much more on this topic in The Health Advocate's Basic Marketing Handbook.

understand the differences, realize that even if they don't like sales, they can still like marketing.)

Now, take a look at all the marketing you do, and commit each marketing task, tactic, decision and choice to one of those pieces of paper or the other.

If you have trouble thinking of them, then ask yourself these questions:

What am I doing well to market my business? What do I like to do, what am I good at, and what has successfully brought new clients to my practice? Add these to your STRENGTHs.

Then, ask yourself:

What am I not doing well for marketing my business? What do I know would work, but my reluctance stands in my way? Or, what don't I have the budget for that I wish I could pay for? What do I know I should be doing on a regular basis, but keeps moving to the bottom of my to-do list? The answers belong, of course, on your WEAKNESSES page.

You might think about it chronologically, or perhaps by how much it cost you (most expensive to least expensive, or vice versa. Go back through the bills you've paid for review.) If you need reminders for the marketing you've done, you might go back through your calendar or your email. Or, consider each of your clients and how they knew to contact you. You can also go through the many tactics listed in *The Health Advocate's Basic Marketing Handbook* to jog your memory on what you have, or haven't yet tried. If you have actually kept a list of all the marketing you've done, then you can add your list keeping to your list of strengths – that's impressive! (Not to mention good business practice.)

It's possible you'll remember something that isn't so black and white as a strength or a weakness. Maybe you ran an ad for new clients, and even though you didn't end up with any contracts, you did get a phone call from the local Lions Club asking you to speak at a lunch meeting. While it was a failure on the one hand, it was a success on the other. It needs to be represented on your list, so I suggest you add it to both lists.

Don't worry about making this neat, or pretty, or even elaborating about the items on your list. This is for your use only, and you need only memory joggers to remind you of the good and not-so-good of your marketing and marketing capability so far.

In total, you may have just a few items on each list – or dozens. When you're satisfied you've covered your strengths and weaknesses, set those lists aside, and take out two new sheets of paper (save trees and use your computer).

At the top of each write   OPPORTUNITIES   and   THREATS

These lists may be a little more difficult to develop because they aren't about you and your work, they are about your observations of the world around you. They summarize all those external factors that either make your marketing easier, or more difficult, that you can either take advantage of, or that you must work around to be successful.

They answer the questions: What is going on "out there" that I can take advantage of to promote my business?

...and...

What is going on "out there" that will threaten my ability to grow and prosper, that require me to develop a marketing response to minimize the threat?

Examples of marketing opportunities might be the fact that open enrollment is coming up soon and you provide insurance reviews, or that a local builder has broken ground for a 55+ townhome community and you have friends who plan to move there. In general, implementation of the Affordable Care Act is an opportunity for all health advocates, so that belongs on your list. Opportunities abound online for promoting your advocacy. Another opportunity might be an invitation to address a group of worker's comp attorneys.

Threats are those outside problems that make us cringe and may prevent our success. They are often pervasive enough that they don't have a negative effect simply on our marketing, but also on our core business. An easy-to-understand (non-advocacy) example of a serious threat was experienced in recent years by some big name corporations and their too-slow reaction to advances in technology. Smith Corona and Kodak didn't take a close enough look at improving technology, nor did they implement changes to their businesses and marketing to accommodate for it. Playing ostrich cost those corporations and many other businesses their stockholders, and their employees lost their jobs. This is why, as uncomfortable as it might seem, it's important to make the analysis of threats. You don't want them blindsiding you, and putting you out of business.

An example of an advocacy practice's threat is finding out you have direct competitors who price their services just a little bit less than you price yours.[5] Another threat would be if your local hospital has implemented a policy that no outside advocates are allowed by patients' bedsides. Still another threat might be learning that the cloud storage you use for your clients' records is at risk of being hacked.

Remember, as you list your SWOTs, that it's not the fact of a strength, weakness, opportunity or threat's existence. It's an assessment of how that threat or opportunity impacts your marketing.

How to Use Your SWOT Lists

If you are like many advocates, you may have an emotional reaction to creating these lists. For some of what you record, you'll be smiling, patting yourself on the back, realizing with some triumph that hey! You're pretty good at this marketing stuff!

---

5   Lower pricing is not a good marketing strategy. There is a discussion of this in *The Health Advocate's Start and Grow Your Own Practice Handbook.*

Just a warning! Don't let the good news of your Strengths result in resting on your laurels. Yes, they represent the "good news" but that doesn't mean you can now set them on a shelf and not pay attention. You must continue to nurture them so they will remain on your strengths list.

On the flip side, don't let your Weaknesses make you wonder what on earth you're doing in business for yourself. Resist your inner Debbie Downer! The smartest business owners (I'll even go out on a limb and say, the happiest people in the world) are those who can look at their own weaknesses as the stage-setters for building their greatest strengths.

Your Opportunities and Threats may trigger some emotions. Of course, Opportunities will set the stage for new ideas for promoting your advocacy. They may be so exciting that they become overwhelming. Threats, by virtue of the fact that they are out of your control, may simply paralyze you and make you fearful of taking the wrong steps.

The key is to be sure that none of your listed items, separately or in total, stop you from moving forward. The difference between a successful business owner, and one who fails, often stems from their answers to "what if?" If "what if?" causes you to stop in your tracks, then you may not succeed. If those two words spur you into action instead, then you have a far better chance of growing your business in the directions you'd like it to grow.

Spur into action – how?

There are two ways we're going to use your SWOT lists to help you figure out what directions to take and, in turn, help you get the most from this book.

EXERCISE– Setting Priorities

The second step in our Marketing SWOT analysis will be to set some priorities. Whether you do this on paper or electronically, we're going to use highlighters to separate them into four different categories.

(Important! Before you get started on this, make a copy (or copies) of each of your four sheets. You're going to mark them up in different ways, and you may change your mind over time about what item should be marketed in what way. Whether you make paper copies, or do a "save as" electronically, don't begin this exercise until you have one or more backups of each page.)

As you work on this exercise, you may wonder why I've recommended specific colors. I did so because there is some psychology to these colors. You'll be highlighting items with like colors from all four lists, regardless of which list they are currently found on.

Orange: Let's first eliminate those things you really can't do anything about. They will be mostly found on your Threats list. These are things you not only can't control, but you feel as if you can't even do something to compete or combat against it.

Yellow: (bright, cheerful, sunny, happy!) Now let's look at those items that are already successful, don't need much (if any) adjustment, and which you can continue to handle exactly as you have been handling it. Most of these will be found on your Strengths list.

Blue: (sad, cold, passive) This will be another elimination color. Highlight in blue any of the items that you really just cannot do or cannot deal with. Maybe you just cannot possibly stand up in front of a large group of people to do public speaking. Maybe you know you could benefit from advertising your services in a local health magazine, but you can't afford to do so. Likewise, you know you aren't a good writer, so blogging or writing articles isn't something you can do well. These items are probably listed on your Weaknesses page, and maybe on your Opportunities page, too even if you can't see your way clear just now to use them as opportunities.

Green: (growing, organic, lush, thriving, go!) You guessed it. Use the green highlighter for those things that are opportunities, even weaknesses, that if you knew more about them, or could develop some confidence in them, or if someone could just teach you HOW, you could begin using them. Maybe you'd like to place an ad, but you don't want to waste your money because you don't know what you should be looking for. Or maybe you would be willing to invest some time in social media, but don't want to waste your time doing it wrong. Go ahead and highlight all those items that you have a willingness to consider doing something about.

You may have figured out why these colors are meaningful and where we're going to go from here.

- Ignore the orange ones – there's nothing you can do about them. (I actually wanted you to use gray, but who has a gray highlighter?)

- Let the yellow ones keep working for you.

- You're going to focus on the green ones to master first. (Green for Go!)

- Then you're going to begin moving some of the blue ones to the green list. (Thus your copies.)

EXERCISE– Honing Your Priorities

Using your green list, assign them numbers or letters to decide which ones you're going to attempt first, then next, then last. You can number them 1, 2, 3 and so forth. Or you can assign a 1 or the letter A to all the ones you think you'd like to try first, then a 2 or B to the next group – however you like to work.

You now have an outline, a direction to take to maximize your marketing outreach – a roadmap for acquiring more clients, specifically more of the right kind of clients. It will help you set some of your green and blue items in motion.

How Often Should You Do a Marketing SWOT Analysis?

Our world and our businesses change all the time. From your movement toward developing a niche, to new legislation that affects healthcare or payment, to hiring or contracting with additional advocates, to expanding your business and more, inside and outside forces will cause you to make adjustments all the time.

Recognizing how much things change, I recommend you review and update your SWOT analysis either once every six months, or with every major change to your business (change in personnel, new niche, etc). This should go hand-in-hand with your review of your marketing plan; in fact, each one should affect the other.

So, now we have some directions to take. Let's make sure we have your ducks lined up, so you are ready to take them on.

We'll start by maximizing your branding and what it can do to support your efforts.

Chapter Two

Strategy: Making Your Brand Work Harder for You

If you think I'm going to suggest you change your logo or your colors or your company's graphical representation as the way to make your brand work harder for you, well, no, I'm not.

Your brand isn't just about a logo or colors or an image. That's only a representation, a trigger for the world to see.

But the real brand itself, the important part, is what that image triggers. It's about behavior and promises, and how well those align with expectations.

That's a big concept – so let's break it down.

Understanding What a Brand Really Is

Here is a logo. What does it mean to you?

Probably nothing. It doesn't represent anything familiar. It doesn't say anything to you because you have no experience with it. It's half a loop with a large dot inside it. That's nice. Big deal.

Here is a logo that is very close to the one above, just turned upside down, minus the dot. What does this one mean to you?

Of course you know this one. It's recognized the world over. It means something. Besides the company name that comes to mind, it also means sports, fun, hard work, athleticism, muscles, sweat, good health and much more. In fact, the word used to describe it, a "swoosh," now includes the name of the company it represents in its definition. Really! Look it up!

But how do you know that? How could a few black pixels on a piece of white paper actually have meaning that isn't spelled out in words?

That's exactly the point. Nike has done the hard, consistent, informational, brand supportive work required to make sure you know exactly what that swoosh means: sports, fun, hard work, athleticism, muscles, or sweat, so that when you are ready to spend money on any of those ideas, Nike will come to mind.

And, it's not just the swoosh. It's the tagline (positioning statement) too.[6] Because if I say, "Just do it!" you know exactly what company I'm talking about too. The same one.

That's what the brand is: a series of triggers that align a person or organization with preconceived promises.

Promises? Yes. Because without meaning to those words, the brand can't do us much good.

Your Brand Promise

Nike already has dibs on concepts (their promises) such as: sports, fun, hard work, athleticism, muscles, or sweat. Not that other businesses, like ours, can't promise those things. But as health advocates, our intent is not to compete with Nike anyway.

Instead, as health advocates, we're focused on other concepts – different promises. Since you have already done the hard work to develop your messages, is should be fairly easy to develop your brand promises, too, since they are mostly interchangeable.

Here are some examples of promises you might want to align with your brand:

Remember, these are concepts that you hope will be triggered when someone sees your logo, hears your name, or your company's name:

- We provide peace of mind

- We can help reduce your medical bills

- We will listen to you

- We will take some of the fear out of your medical experience

- We'll help you make the right choices for yourself

- We'll facilitate your work with your physicians

- We'll help you or your family

---

6   Learn more about taglines and positioning statements in *The Health Advocate's Basic Marketing Handbook*.

There are dozens of other concepts / promises you might choose from. There are also modifiers that go with them, relating to how you will make those promises happen, such as:

- We'll perform these services with a high level of quality
- We'll perform them quickly
- We'll perform them based on your needs
- We'll charge you a fair price
- We'll perform services wearing blue plaid with green polka dots (OK, not really, just want to be sure you are paying attention.)
- We'll be sure there are no conflicts of interest when we perform our services
- … or many others, too, of course.

The point to the modifiers is to make sure people understand your standards; not just that you'll take care of them, but the care you take to do so, too.

The question now is how to make sure people align your logo, tagline, colors and other images they might recognize with your promises. What will help them make that leap from images and taglines to a real understanding of what you do and how you can help them?

How Do We Align a Brand with Its Promises?

Aligning your brand with its promises can't and won't happen overnight, or just because you say they should align.

Instead, that alignment develops over time, through your own efforts. The more effort you make, the sooner your brand begins to stand for something – hopefully those promises you want it to stand for. Unless you make a concerted effort, your brand and its promises may never sync at all.

This is actually quite simple to understand. To do so, let's look at political candidates. Have you ever gone to the polls on election day only to see a name of someone running for office that you don't recognize? That candidate stands for something, certainly, or she wouldn't be running for office, right? But if you haven't been exposed to her brand, if you don't know what she stands for, then why would you vote for her? Further, because your vote is so important, and will affect the future of your town, or region, or state, would you simply take a chance and vote for her? What if you found out later that she believes just the opposite of what you believe?

Potential clients want and need to know exactly what you and your brand stand for. They aren't going to "vote" for you unless they do know and understand that you represent what they want and need. That means it's up to you to make it really obvious what they can expect from you – what your brand promises.

Many advocates hire a designer to create their logo, maybe help them choose a name, design a webpage and some business cards... Then they wait for the phone to ring. Then they don't understand why it doesn't ring, because, after all, they've created their brand.

The step they missed, of course, was this alignment of brand and promises. By missing the step, they may find themselves out of business.

So, how do you take the step? How do you facilitate that alignment between brand, promises and getting hired?

Through marketing, of course. Lots of marketing. Using the tactics outlined in both *The Health Advocate's Basic Marketing Handbook* and this book. And now you understand why that's so important.

The more marketing you do, including the important customer service aspects of your work (Chapter Six), the faster your brand will align with its promises in the minds of your target audiences.

That is, as long as you don't violate your brand and ruin its perception.

The Brand Perception Paradox

It's true in life, and it's true in branding. That is, that our perceptions are our reality. Or, as Momma used to say, "Actions speak louder than words." Or, as Trisha says, "Actions speak louder than your strategic brand promise."

This is a branding paradox because the purpose of branding is to control the message. And yet, your brand messages may not be received the same way they are issued, meaning you have lost control.

Here's an example:

In all your marketing materials you have made it very clear that you will be a partner with your clients, and that you are a facilitator - that you'll help them communicate with their doctors to help them get what they need from the system. You have also done some public speaking where you work in those messages – your intended brand promises – and it says the same thing all over your website. All good!

So Mrs. Hannigan calls you. She is upset because her husband is having strange symptoms, and after two visits to his doctor she feels as if the doctor just won't listen to her or her husband. She wants to know whether you can help her. She found your website and it says that's your area of service, but can you help HER and HIM?

Yes! You tell her, you can help! In fact, you've helped others in similar situations, whereupon you launch into a handful of stories about other people you have helped in a similar fashion... 30 minutes later you hang up the phone and never hear from Mrs. Hannigan again.

What happened?

What happened is that Mrs. Hannigan's perception of your brand based on the promises you made in your brochure and on your website, and the reality of the phone call with you, caused a disconnect. She told you what she thought the problem was, and then you spent the next 25 minutes bending her ear about other people.

She didn't call to get her ear bent. She called because she wanted someone to listen to HER, and not the other way around. She even told you, "The doctor won't listen to either of us." That could have been your clue to do that – listen – showing her you could provide what she needed.

Now her perception of your brand, and you, has nothing to do with all that effort you have put into your marketing. Instead her perception is based on her one experience, and that is, that you talk too much and you don't listen. Ouch.

And yet, maybe she really did understand your brand promise. Maybe you weren't promising to listen. Maybe you were promising to be the expert who does all the talking, no matter what you thought your promise meant.

Your brand promises will evolve constantly. Every time you do new marketing, and every time a potential client recognizes your brand, it will cement the meaning of your promises – whether or not they are the promises you intended.

That's why you must be very clear in what you promise, and be just as clear in your delivery, making sure those two are aligned.

Shades of Branding Gray

Later in this book we'll identify some new and different kinds of target audiences. As we learned in the *Basic Marketing Handbook*, different target audiences may have different interests in the work you do. With different interests comes the need for different promises.

This is easier done than said. (Yes – you read that right!) When you develop your brand and your promises (messages) you simply make sure they are relevant for the audience you want to influence to work with you.

For example, if your audience is an adult child with a sick, elderly parent, your brand promises will be about the relief and peace of mind you provide. If another audience is people whose hospital bills are too high, your brand should reflect your ability to negotiate well.

But how do you know who will see and experience your brand? How can you be sure the right nuances are built in for different audiences?

If your audiences have similar interests in your work, and expect a similar type of experience from you, then just keep your branding broad enough that it will suffice for all of them. So, for example, if you offer broad advocacy services to people of any age with any sort of medical navigational need, then your messages can be those broad promises mentioned earlier in this chapter.

But sometimes your audiences will vary quite a bit. Maybe you work with individuals, but you access them through their employers, or through their unions. Or perhaps your clientele mostly comes through a relationship with trust attorneys, even though the work you do is reviewing and reducing medical bills.

Employers, attorneys, individuals with outrageous medical bills – they all have very different needs when it comes to the brand messages they seek. We won't cover the specific messages here (because we'll discuss them in Chapter Five) but know that your brand can reflect them. For example, you can use the same images across all your marketing materials, but can adjust the text according to the needs of each audience. That might mean you develop a new brochure for each audience, or you have a different web page for each. But the logo and colors that represent your promises can remain the same.

Or you can do variations on a theme. A good example of this is FedEx. The outline of the letters of the company name remain the same, but their colors change to reflect the differences in services. If you want overnight delivery, the logo is orange and purple. If you want ground delivery, the logo is purple and green. If you need customer services, you'll find them being handled with a logo that is purple and blue. In all cases, the brand promise is that your package will be delivered in exactly the manner you need it to be delivered, based on the choices you make.

If you think your brand promises will need some sort of distinction in their delivery, you might also want to consider variations on your logo and color schemes.

Brand Loyalty

Brand loyalty is exactly what it sounds like – customers return to the same brand over and over again as long as their promises are fulfilled and they need to avail themselves of the promises being made. They keep spending their money on a product or service of a certain brand because they have come to **trust** it. <- Note that very important word: trust. We'll return to it many times in the course of this book.

Brand loyalty is business and marketing nirvana! It's the equilibrium sought after by every business. It means customers and clients don't even think about their choices. They make them almost subconsciously because they know what to expect and they want what they know. Brand loyalty makes the choosing so easy that they just automatically gravitate to it.

Creating so much loyalty among your clients should be your goal too. The closer your brand promises are to the actual delivery of your work, the better chance your clients will be loyal to you. Even better, they will become so trusting of that allegiance between your promises and your delivery that they want others to benefit by working with you as well.

However, a caution about brand loyalty is in order here. That is, it is way too simple to lose that loyalty. The minute you operate outside your promises, that trust will begin to erode. If your violation of that trust is too large, you'll lose loyalty all together.

Think of this in the simpler terms of the grocery store. Maybe you prefer the brand name mayonnaise, but when it's time to buy it, you find that not only has the price gone up, but the 32 ounce quart is now only 28 ounces! Or that box of branded granola that has always been a favorite no longer has raisins in it. "What gives?" you wonder... which now makes you pause (which you never would have done if YOUR mayonnaise and YOUR granola had been available...) And just for grins and chuckles, you try another brand, or even the store brand.

They violated your trust, and now you've yielded your loyalty.

It's one thing if it's a few ounces of food that would be consumed and replaced in a week. It's another thing if trust is lost for an advocate who could save a life, or a life savings.

Encourage brand loyalty by maintaining your promises, and therefore your clients' trust. Never violate that trust if possible, and if you think that could possibly happen, be sure to let your clients know what might be different – manage their expectations before they stop trusting you.

No small business can intentionally violate its clients' trust, and therefore its brand loyalty. Nor can a business take that trust for granted.

Building Brand Equity

If you intend to sell your practice at the end of a period of time, there is even more reason to concentrate on building a strong brand. That's because a well-recognized, positive, loyalty-inducing brand can make your business worth more financially.

Brand equity, the amount of money your brand is worth, is very difficult to quantify by itself. Rarely would anyone, a buyer, seller or broker, be able to put a specific price on it, especially in our profession that has such a short track record.

Instead it becomes a multiplier or a modifier. Pricing a business for sale is usually described as a function of x times your average income over x number of years. But when you have a strong brand, it will make your business worth much more. And if you have a negative brand, it will reduce the value of your business, and you'll take a hit on its sale (if you can sell it at all.)

Here are two examples:

> Think of Facebook - a free service. With no profit yet on the books, when its stock went public (meaning, part of it was for sale), it was worth a billion dollars. The ONLY thing Facebook had to sell was its name, its brand. The Facebook brand was known the world over. Not everyone had positive feelings about it! But advertisers did – and thus, Facebook's brand promise of delivering more eyeballs to advertisers than any other brand in the world was recognized as being worth a billion dollars.

> Now think of Chevrolet. In 2012, Chevy was still "As American as baseball, hot dogs, apple pie and Chevrolet." Its stock was always a good one to have in your portfolio because there was so much value to the brand. And then, beginning in late 2013, over the course of the next year, millions upon millions of Chevys were recalled because of a problem in the mechanics. The evening news featured the families of Chevy drivers who had died because Chevy didn't address the problems, instead sweeping them under the rug, hoping customers wouldn't connect its brand with its killer mechanics. Chevrolet stock - and sales - tanked.

What is important to note here is that these two brands, as iconic as any brands that exist today, saw their value affected by brand promises alone. In both cases, those promises were not about their words, not about what they said their brands were supposed to represent. In both cases, the brands were valued based on their actions – which, yes – spoke far louder than their words.

The lesson for any business owner is to understand that your brand has value for both the acquisition of new clients, and for the long term value of your business too. That makes it imperative that you treat your brand with TLC, that you birth it well, nurture it, strengthen it, build its loyalty, and appreciate it, in word and in deed.

Now that we better understand branding, promises, trust and loyalty, let's take a look at how we can hone in more closely on the core of our work – our niche within the marketplace.

Chapter Three

Strategy: Developing Your Market Niche

Every profession has generalists and specialists:

- In medicine we find primary care providers. We also find specialists in certain diseases, body systems, treatments and even age groups.

- In the law, we find general lawyers, plus specialty law practices like litigation, criminal law, corporate law, wills and estates, immigration and others.

- Hairdressers (or barbers) might focus on one gender or another, or a type of hair (like black hair), and some specialize in use of products from only one manufacturer.

- Accountants might do general corporate accounting work within a large office full of accountants, or as one of a small team working in another type of business. Or maybe they focus only on income tax management and returns.

In all those cases, the professionals who have moved their practices into a subset or segment of a larger audience have determined a niche. As private advocacy continues to grow and becomes more widely known, niches are developing in our profession as well.

If you provide "general advocacy services" that means you support patients and caregivers who need your help, regardless of who they are or what kind of help they need. Even if they require services you can't provide, you'll find someone to help them, perhaps working with strategic partners.

However, you may choose a different approach to your work. Maybe you prefer to work only with senior-aged people, or maybe you want to support only patients who rely on alternative therapies. Maybe your passion is helping women with breast cancer, or children with psychiatric conditions. Or maybe you've learned that medical billing is the only part of your work that excites you, so you focus your marketing on that. Those segments are all considered niche services.

Choosing to stay a generalist, or creating a niche for your work—neither is necessarily preferable to the other. The question is not which you prefer. Rather, if you think you'd like to develop a niche, you need to make sure your marketplace can support it.

Two Roads May Lead You to a Niche...

If you are considering focusing your advocacy practice on a specific niche, there are two ways to determine what it should be.

In the first scenario, you have specific interest and experience in performing those niche services. For example, you may have spent a career as an oncology nurse, or maybe you've shepherded family members through cancer diagnoses and treatment – and now you think you'd like to focus your advocacy on cancer patients.

That is a road made of pre-existing skills combined with your specific interest.

In the second scenario, you start your work as a generalist, but you realize that you have one or two favorite kinds of clients or types of work, or perhaps you figure out that a certain type of case is more lucrative than others, so you begin to move your practice toward that one niche.

This type of niche is market-driven. You didn't start your work with that focus, but close attention to your marketplace and how it affects you and your practice has led you in that direction.

...But Only One of Those Roads Will Lead to Success

The truth is, no matter how you determine what your niche will be, you cannot be successful unless your market recognizes it, appreciates it, and hires you for it.

It's not good enough that you have experience and wishes for your business. The reality is that unless your audiences are willing to pay you for the work, and there are enough clients who need those services, then your skills and interests won't be enough.

The good news is that most of the time, if your niche has been well thought-out and enough of your audience is within your geographic reach, then you can probably entice audiences to pay you for what you want to do – for working within your niche.

The best way to understand this is by example:

> Nancy worked as a nurse in a breast cancer doctor's office for many years. Then she, herself, was diagnosed with breast cancer. She successfully completed treatment, but just could not face returning to work in her old office. Her own experience taught her that sometimes patients weren't getting all the guidance they needed. Further, she suffered her own difficulties with getting questions answered, and getting her insurer to cooperate. She understood, as she never had before, that patients aren't as well-served as they could be by the system. So Nancy decided to start a new advocacy practice focused on breast cancer patients. Her years of experience on the provider side, and her own experience on the patient side made this niche perfect for her practice.

I expect you're thinking, "what a good idea!" We know there are thousands of breast cancer patients who can use her expertise to smooth their paths through a breast cancer diagnosis, right? Surely she was successful!

But no. You might be surprised to learn that Nancy's practice failed. She only worked with three clients in her first year of business and could not sustain a practice with so few.

Why did her practice fail? We can easily cite two reasons.

First, Nancy took all the important steps necessary to get her practice up and running, including marketing her services. But she didn't spend enough time learning about target audiences and benefits. As a result of the marketing she did, the calls she got weren't about breast cancer; they were about many services an advocacy generalist might provide. Had Nancy focused her marketing properly, she might have been successful.

Secondly, instead of following her market and helping those who did call her, Nancy simply dismissed them. "I'm sorry, I only work with breast cancer patients. I can't help you."

Nancy struck out in both directions.

The Goldilocks Approach to Niche Development

Clearly what Nancy needed was a far more balanced approach – one that was just right.

First, she needed to hone in on her market much more clearly. She needed to focus her marketing on women, or the partners who love them. Her messages needed to clearly outline the benefits of working with her. Instead she ran some random ads in her weekly community newspaper that just gave her company name and a phone number and email address. Even her website doesn't say much about breast cancer, or her work or personal experience.

Secondly, Nancy needed to listen carefully to the people who called her. The very fact that they were asking her to provide services she wasn't prepared to provide should have told her two things: that she might want to consider expanding the services she offered (because clearly there are people who would hire her for those other services) – and – that her marketing needed to be clearer if she wanted those phone calls to come in from breast cancer patients or their caregivers.

In both cases, Nancy was simply asleep at the switch. An understanding of basic marketing, the very roots of audiences and messages, would have saved her from the first mistake. And the simplest of customer service and quality improvement would have saved her from the second.

If you hope to develop a niche for your practice, you'll need to be more Goldilocks in your approach – you'll need the one that's balanced, and just right.

How to Develop Your Niche

So let's assume you don't want to fail like Nancy did (a safe assumption, I'm sure!).... Here are some steps to take to begin developing a niche within your own practice.

I say "some steps," because this is just an overview. There are entire books written to help business owners create niches within their marketplaces. You'll get some basics here, and if you want to know more, I encourage you to either work with a marketing professional, or to read further. Find resources in the ORB. ORB

So let's get started:

Creating a successful niche within advocacy requires a balance among four things: what you like to do, what you are good at doing, development of authority and trust, and what people are willing to pay you to do.

Let their nexus define your niche.

• What do you like to do?

If you won the billion dollar lottery but wanted to keep on working, what kinds of patients or challenges would you want to work with? If you can answer that question, then you know what work you like to do and a direction you could take an advocacy niche.

Do you prefer working with one age group more than another? (Say, the elderly, or children.) Or would you want to focus on one gender? Maybe you have experience and a deep interest in one group of diseases, like cancer or dementias.

Don't sweat this question. If you have preferences, you have them. If you don't, don't worry about it because if you decide to build a niche, you can do so later based on where the market takes you.

• What are you good at?

This question is tougher for many advocates because they hate that whole "toot your own horn" approach to saying what they are good at. But as a business owner, you must learn to talk openly about your strengths. It goes with owning a business.

Within the entire spectrum of services a patient or health advocate might offer, what are your strengths? Are you good with certain ages of people? Do you know a lot about arthritis? Can you whip a hospital bill into shape and knock those billing department bullies to their knees when it comes to negotiating?

Take a look at the master list of services being offered today by private advocates and see which ones you've already conquered.[7] You might add those you know enough to get started with.

But be frank and honest. Ask yourself, "Would I pay me to perform this service?"

If the answer is no, but you still want to be able to get paid for doing that work, you'll need to learn a lot more about it before you can decide it should be your niche.

• Are you an authority? Do people trust you to perform these specific services?

Being good at something, and being recognized as an expert, are two different things. In order to build a niche for your business, it requires you be trusted to perform those

---

7   http://www.advoconnection.com/services.htm

specific services – that they be your reputation, your brand. To understand this point the best, read through Chapter Two about branding carefully. It's about promises and trust.

• **Will people pay you for these niche services?**

Marketing aside, because marketing is just the broadcasting of your ability and the benefits you say you can provide, will potential clients perceive that you are worthy of being paid to help them within your niche?

Remember – this isn't about whether you are capable. It's about the perception that you are not only capable, but worth paying for. It goes beyond trust. It goes to the heart of who they are – able and willing to pay you for the work.

The real key to figuring out the answer to this question will rely on market research. For patient advocacy generalists, I've not written or advised much on doing market research because the population of people who need and can afford to pay for advocacy services is huge. There aren't nearly enough advocates for all the people who need them and are willing to pay for them, no matter where you live.

But the more targeted and tailored your desired niche, the more likely it is that you'll need to do some market research to figure out if there are enough people who will need your niche services who can also afford to pay for them.

We aren't going to cover market research here. It was covered in *The Health Advocate's Basic Marketing Handbook*[8] I and I have provided additional resources in the ORB. **ORB**

Just know that to give yourself the best chance of market niche success, and to save yourself grief and money, doing that research will give you a good start on the answer to the question about whether or not there will be enough people to pay you to do the work you want to do.

Finally, as you get started in your niche, you may want to assume that people will be reluctant to pay you for this specific work, or at least that not enough people will be willing to do so. That may or may not be true, but use it as a platform for building your niche-focused marketing. By assuming they can't or won't pay you, you'll work harder at developing the messages and tools you'll need to attract them.

Niche Marketing Isn't Rocket Science

.... At least no more than any other form of marketing. There is no difference – NONE – between marketing your niche services and marketing general advocacy services. It's simply tailored to fit the specific audiences you need to speak to, those who will contract with you to help them.

To be most successful in the shortest period of time with your niche marketing will require extra emphasis on two aspects of your marketing: first, creating your brand promises to focus on your niche, and second, building your own expertise to support your niche.

---

8 *The Health Advocate's Basic Marketing Handbook:* Chapter Thirteen (Section 1, Part II: Market and Situation Analysis)

The topic of branding and its promises is covered in Chapter Two. The topic of developing your reputation as an expert is covered in Chapter Four.

A Few More Niche Development and Marketing Guidelines

- Don't be afraid to say no. That seems both frightening and counterintuitive to many new advocates, but those who have been in business for a while see the merit in the ability to turn away a potential client who doesn't fit the parameters of their work. If someone calls and asks you, the patient advocate, to help them get their car repaired, then you know that's not within the boundaries of your work product. It's easy to say no.

  Developing a niche will require you to say no even when something seems to – mostly – fit. If your niche is working with people's hospital bills, and they phone you with a problem with doctor's office bill – will you say yes or no? If your niche is hospital bills, then you may decide to say no – or risk losing control of your niche boundaries. That might even turn you into a generalist again.

- However... you should never totally reject a potential client or caller. There's a big difference between saying, "I can't help you" and "I can't help you, but here's a resource for finding the help you need." The second answer is far more professional. If you don't know of someone else who can help out, you can always refer callers to the AdvoConnection Directory.[9]

- Don't get too specific with your niche. Focusing your work on older people is a good niche. Focusing it on older people with dementia might also work. But if you focus it on people who live in a town with a population of only 2,000 people, that is probably way too narrow. There won't be enough business to keep you in business.

- It's OK to focus on more than one niche at a time. The key here may not be how many niches you choose; rather how well related they are. For example, Chick-Fil -A has developed a niche with – yes – chicken. If they began serving shrimp tacos, it would be a huge stretch to get people to order them because they've built a reputation on something else entirely. But it wouldn't be such a big stretch for them to begin selling chicken tacos because they are made from – yes – chicken.

  This will be true with your advocacy niche(s) too.

Finding your success within a specific niche may take a little longer than building a practice that offers general advocacy services, but if you know for sure there is a big enough audience (through your market research) and you are able to brand your work and create your aura of expertise, then eventually you may find more success than general advocacy might have provided.

So let's look next at developing that aura of expertise.

---

9   http://www.AdvoConnection.com
     Learn more about this basic customer service tenet in Chapter Six of this book.

Chapter Four

Strategy:
Becoming a Recognized Expert
(Expanding Your Personal Brand)

I am an expert in patient empowerment and the business of health advocacy.

There – I said it. Please notice that the earth didn't move, and my mother (who taught me never to brag) didn't turn over in her grave.

As recently as 2004, I wasn't an expert, at least as far as the healthcare system, patient empowerment or advocacy were concerned. My story of why I got involved in any of this work has been told many times, and won't be retold here. But the upshot is that I had a horrible experience, I made lemonade out of it, and here I am today writing my fourth book, having successfully created my "aura of expertness".

Note that does not say "aura of expertise". It says "expertness" which is different.

There's actually quite a gap between your expertise and your aura of expertness....

Expertise is...	Expertness is...
Your knowledge and skill set – your competency. It's internal, known only to you.	The recognition by other people of that expertise. It's external. It describes their respectful (sometimes awed) regard for your level of knowledge and skill. It's your authority and your personal brand.
Developed by continually building your knowledge and competency levels.	The aura of being an expert, the public regard for your expertise, authority and personal brand is a function of good marketing. It comes from other people and their respect and description of you, based on your behavior.

Which is why this is being addressed in a marketing book. To be a recognized expert, you'll need to conquer that gap, and you'll do so by marketing yourself as a thought leader and an expert.

A Personal Story of Becoming a Recognized Expert

In Spring of 2004, I didn't know squat about the healthcare system. Nothing. I'd birthed a couple of babies and later undergone a hysterectomy, but I was a marketing consultant who didn't even have any healthcare clients. When it came to knowing how to get what I needed from the system, I was a babe in the woods.

Three years later, by 2007, I was writing my Every Patient's Advocate newspaper column, hosting a health-related radio show, and was the patient empowerment expert for About.com, owned then by the New York Times.

Of course, the catalyst for my change in careers was my horrible odyssey through the world of misdiagnosis which sparked an interest I never could have anticipated; that is, learning the inner workings of the medical system, and crafting tactics to help patients get what we need from it. (http://everypatientsadvocate.com/misdiagnosis.htm)

How did I do that in such a short period of time?   I went to school.

No, not in the classic ivy-covered building version. My schooling was all self-taught. I read everything I could get my hands on – books, articles, even medical journal articles that were on topic. I interviewed hundreds of people, from doctors, nurses and other practitioners, to EMTs, urgent care administrators and pharmacists. And I listened, carefully, to the complaints and problems expressed by hundreds of patients and caregivers who had found hiccups, challenges and brick walls as they tried to journey successfully through the system.

The more I read and interviewed, the more I was also led into a new world of other experts, mostly self-made like myself, who had suffered at the hands of the healthcare system. They had lost loved ones to medical mistakes, from surgery gone bad, to hospital infections, to drug mistakes and more.

I'm still in "school" every day. I still read voraciously on these topics. I discuss my passion with new people daily.

If I had to put my finger on the one most important thing I've done to develop my expertise, it is to keep an open mind. Granted, I do a lot of writing, and a lot of formulating of tools and tactics. But every one of them has evolved from listening and learning – and being willing to adjust as I went along.

I share all of this with you to show you that you can become an expert in a subject area you know almost nothing about in a very short time. You will need to put your blood, sweat and tears into it. But yes, it can be done.

If I had asked myself in 2004 or even 2005 whether I'd be willing to pay ME to advise on patient empowerment topics, I would have answered, "no!" But as I write to you today, 10 years later, that I am, indeed, an expert. And that paying me a premium for patient empowerment advice (and advocacy business advice too!) is worth it.

Why Be THE Expert?

Because you are a professional with a skill set that should be recognized as such. You not only deserve to be respected for that level of knowledge and skill, but you should also be rewarded for it. Your reward can be not just professional success, but professional-level "uber-respect" as well. As the thought leader, the authority, the trusted source, you will be invited to speak, your audiences will be happy to read your blog or buy a book you publish, they will hire you for your advocacy skills, and they will pay you more because you are an authority.

This last point should not be undersold. Once other people regard you as an expert, it can make a huge difference in your income. Experts can command higher income. (More in the sidebar below.)

While most marketing is considered proactive and "push" (meaning, you do things to get in someone's face to remind them you exist – advertising, public relations, billboards, etc), you as an expert actually end up with the ability to "pull" people toward you. People will seek you out more often than just when they need your services. They will look for your opinion on topics of interest. They will assign more importance to what you have to say than they otherwise might. They will go in search of you rather than waiting for you to be in their faces.

No longer will you promote your expertise in the same ways you do when you began. Awareness of you and your expertise will mean people come looking for you, the authority, instead of vice-versa. Not that you won't have to market your services anymore. Just that you will now need to provide reminders rather than new information.)

You know, the standard line we all use, "They say (this)" or "They say (that)."?

As an expert, you will be "they!"

That said, being recognized as an expert isn't for everyone. This is not a "must do" for marketing a patient advocacy practice. It can be an enormous boost to your marketing, and will be well worth your effort because you'll be able to command more money, too. But if you choose not to go the expert route, it won't have a detrimental effect on your practice.

Making More Money as an Expert

What is the difference between Ralph Lauren and Dom Streater? They are both clothing designers, but which one do you think makes more money?

What is the difference between Michelle Bachman and Sandra Adams? Both women have served in the United States Congress, but one is far better known than the other. They probably make the same salary from their day jobs (Congress) but one commands far more money as a public speaker because she is considered a national thought leader (No matter whether you agree with her.) Which one do you think it is?

Or, what is the difference between Wolfgang Puck and Marcel Vigneron? They are both celebrity chefs, but who makes more money based on his personal brand?

Establishing your personal brand as an expert will help you, too, command more money. If you have been diligent about putting yourself "out there" so your potential audiences recognize your authority, then when you tell them what your charges will be for your advocacy work, speaking or any other income streams you have, they will be willing to pay it, even when it's higher than your competitors.

Expertness is Personal, Not Business

Think of the experts you know on any topic. They might be local, or national, or even international...

Every single one of them is a person. Because experts are people, not businesses.

Further, not one of them was born an expert. In every case, they built their expertise, and sought the environment that would regard them as experts – proactively, intentionally, with exactly that goal in mind: to be highly respected in their domain – as experts.

Neither expertise, nor the regard for one's expertise – expertness – just happens. Theirs didn't, and yours won't either. They worked hard to build their personal brands, and you will need to do the same. That requires hard, smart work, good self-esteem, consistency, putting yourself in the right place at the right time, and a smidge (or more) of ego as well.

Because....

Expertness Requires Chutzpah, Passion and a Belief in Yourself

As mentioned earlier, establishing and maintaining your aura of expertness is about being public. It will require you to step up and speak your piece, to be forthright, to be brave, bold and passionate.

In effect, it will require you to ignore what your mother had to say about bragging. If your mom was like mine, you didn't ever dare draw attention yourself or your own abilities and accomplishments. It just wasn't polite.

I promise you, that while it's not easy at first (SO not easy at first!) it does become easier over time. Your biggest hurdle won't be learning the facts you need to learn to be an expert, it will be that first time you make the public statement, perhaps in response to the question, "What do you do for a living?" You'll say, "I'm an expert in _____."

The second time you answer that question, it will be easier. The third easier still. It won't take too many times before it rolls off your tongue (or fingers.) That is how you build your personal brand, including the trust and authority that goes along with it.

The earth won't shake, and Mom won't roll over in her grave because you made that statement either.

I should note here that creating your aura of expertness doesn't mean you'll become famous. It's not like you'll begin showing up on the national news, or called to the Oval Office. Nor will anyone even recognize you at the supermarket. (Although I suppose if you really max out your expertness with something of national importance that could happen!)

For most of us, that's the good news. We don't care about being famous. But we do care what people think of us, how they regard us and our expertise. We are highly passionate about our subject areas and that passion osmoses from every pore. We truly believe that what we are doing is right and good – not just for ourselves but for our clients, too.

The passion for your platform (your subject area) is just as important as your willingness and ability to be forthright about it. Your belief in your work and its ability to improve mankind needs to be as tough as nails.

Most of us experts end up as very big fish in very small ponds. There's plenty of room for big fish in the healthcare / advocacy pond – so I hope you'll want to jump in and join those of us who are already here, even if it's only in your own community. We need your passion because it helps patients get what they need.

It's time, then, to take a look at building your personal brand and establishing your aura of expertise. What does it take to turn you into that recognized expert?

What Makes an Expert?

There are four "P" components to establishing regard for your expertise – your expertness. Being an expert requires you build for yourself a four-legged stool comprised of

- Your platform
- Your profile
- Your pond
- Your public

Each leg supports the other. No one or two of the components can stand on its own. And all must continue to grow together in order to continue supporting each other.

Let's break them down.

• **YOUR PLATFORM** is the environment in which you are an authority – your niche. It's the subject matter where others believe your expertise lies.

- Julia Child was an expert in **French cooking**.
- Jerry Seinfeld is an expert in **comedy**.
- Maya Angelou was an expert in **poetry**.
- Warren Buffet is an expert in **investing**.

Their platforms are/were French cooking, comedy, poetry and investing – definable niches. Within those platforms each person made a name for him or herself, and because they did such a great job building their reputations, we have heard of them, too, even though those may not be areas we know much about.

Platform is a function of perception, and not necessarily reality. Because these experts are/ were so prominent in their fields, we actually assign more regard to them than they might even claim themselves. Some people would say that Julia Childs was an expert in food, even though she might have disputed that, having carved out only a sub-platform, a definable niche of food for her expertise – French cooking. Warren Buffet is perceived by many as being an expert in business, although there are probably many aspects of business he really doesn't know much about, like human resources, or supply chain management.

My platform, what Trisha Torrey is known for, is in how the healthcare system functions, patient empowerment, and the business of patient advocacy. I'm also an expert in sub-platforms within those areas, like doctor-patient communication, or patient safety, or marketing advocacy, and even – apropos of this chapter – turning oneself into an expert.

But people often tell me they regard my expertise as being in healthcare. But that is really only their perception. There are many aspects of healthcare I know nothing about, including the holy grail - medicine!

There are probably more benefits than problems that stem from others broadening what they perceive to be your expertise. As long as you don't promote yourself for something that isn't really your definable niche, and as long as you correct their misperceptions when possible, it shouldn't be a problem.

Your platform will also be the foundation for your income. And, ironically, the smaller, more targeted your platform, the more income you may be able to command. There are lots of books out there about marketing, and lots of books available about marketing service businesses. But how many books do you know of that are written specifically about marketing private advocacy practices? Thus – yes – the books I've written on advocacy business topics, my platform, are very expensive.

The other parts of your platform are the tools you use to share your expertise. It's comprised of what you teach, transmit or share (including opinions and advice when appropriate) and how you share it. Your platform may be a website, social media or a blog. It might be a book you have written, or articles you have published. It could be speeches or talks you have given, classes you have taught, or TV appearances. Whatever modes you use to share your expertise are also a part of your platform.

My platform is shared through books, websites, blogs, social media, workshops and more. For most of us, the more tools we use, the more places and modes people can experience us and our work, the higher the public's esteem – although – it's possible to be in too many places, and show up too much, too....

Because, yes, just like dating, a little bit of "hard to get" might also go a long way.

We'll return to the importance of platform again, but now let's move on to the next leg of our stool.

• **YOUR PROFILE** is the next component of your expertise.

Your profile is exactly what it would seem to be – it's who you are, your background and experience, the expertise you have developed, including for many, the reasons it was developed. It may include your education (or not), your career (or not), or any other aspect of your life that has lent itself to creating who you are – your profile.

If you have been an emergency room nurse for most of your career, then that's part of your profile. Included is your education, everything you learned, your experiences along the way, some of the patients you met and interfaced with, the doctors you worked alongside and more..

If you have been a billing coder for a doctor or a claims processor for a health insurer, you can bet that people regard you as an expert in CPTs and DRGs. Maybe you've also worked for a hospital processing bills or fielding calls from disgruntled patients with bills they thought were too high. If you did all this in a large city, that's part of your profile. If you did it in a very rural area, that could also be part of your profile.

If you have one to tell, a personal story can add to your platform. If you would like your platform to be eldercare, and you were the caregiver for your parents, and one of them had Alzheimer's, then by all means, share your stories. Appropriate stories enhance your authority in the eyes of others who share your platform, and those who are interested in your subject area.

My profile includes my personal story. But it also includes a master's degree, 8 years of classroom teaching, and 20+ years of marketing. My profile is a blend of all these experiences – who I am and what I have achieved – and have culminated in my expertness in ways I never could have imagined if I hadn't been motivated to do something big, intentionally, after my healthcare system fiasco in 2004.

When put together, this all creates your platform, part of your personal brand. Your brand promise will result being authentic – it's the only way you can build trust (see Chapter Two). This isn't something you can fake. It must be real, it must be you, and it must be recognized for the history it is built on.

- The third leg of your stool is your **POND.**

As the expert fish, you'll want to be sure you define your pond well.

Your pond is the geographic area in which you are considered an authority. I am a fish in a patient advocacy and empowerment pond (platform or niche), with a geographic scope that is international (because we have members of the Alliance of Professional Health Advocates who live and work in seven different countries)

But your pond doesn't need to be, and probably shouldn't be, so large. In fact, trying to become a big enough, recognizable fish on a huge pond, one that is national or international in scope, may be a waste of your time if your practice is local or regional.

The best way to determine the size of your pond should be is by clearly defining your niche (Chapter Three), and marrying it to your geography.

For example, if you live and work in Denver and your niche is breast cancer patients, then your pond is just that. You'll want your promotion to focus on breast cancer patients in the general Denver area, or even broadened a little to all of Colorado. It wouldn't do you a lot of good to focus on recognition for your authority in New York, or Miami, or Canada because people who live in those areas aren't going to hire you anyway.

On the other hand, maybe you are a highly skilled medical bill negotiator fish who effectively reduces hospital bills, specifically for surgery patients. Your pond will be broader in its geographic scope because you're willing and able to tackle hospital bills for anyone in the United States.

The key to defining your pond well will be to make it narrow enough to distinguish yourself, but not so narrow that your pond can't grow if you decide to make it bigger later.

I know – easier said than done. Meaning, err on the side of slightly larger, just in case you find yourself with a larger adoring public hoping to swim in your pond, or more fish trying to share your space.

- The fourth and final leg of our expertness stool is **YOUR PUBLIC.**

Your public is your following; the people who care about what you have to say. People who think you can help them, or help them understand, in their time of need or interest.

Without your public, your following, expertness just doesn't exist, no matter how smart, skilled or knowledgeable you are about your subject area. You may still be an expert! You may still have plenty of expertise! But if a tree falls in the forest, and no one is around, well – who cares? If an expert has no following, no public with knowledge of his expertise – well – who cares?

We all have a public of some measure. Friends and family members may be at the tops of our lists. But to be considered a real expert, you'll need to impress and influence others who know you only for your professional capabilities. They may be clients, or co-workers. Or, you may intentionally focus your marketing to rally new additions to your followers.

Creating Your Authority (Expertness)

Now it's time to look at yourself, your interests, your expertise, and your goals, to determine the best approach for creating your own expertness. We're going to look at each leg of our expert stool. I've provided some ideas for you here to get you started on building and strengthening each leg.

Begin with your profile because that's about you, and it's what you know the best.

EXERCISE—Your Credentials

Write down all your experiences, skills, and other attributes that comprise your expertise. Include personal stories, jobs you've had, your education, even your location if it is important. You'll answer the question, "What credentials do you have for being the expert you claim to be?"

It is important to note here that the exercise you have just completed is the least amount of expertise you should ever be able to outline. Your goal will be to stay current with your subject area, and to expand it when desirable or necessary.

Here are some ways to continually build your authority and expertise:

- Find holes in your knowledge and fill them.
- Listen, listen, listen, and read, read, read, Stay as current as you can.
- Observe other experts in your field including your competition, and emulate what works for them.
- Forge relationships and partnerships with others who are not just like-minded, but even those with whom you disagree.
- Work on your communications skills. Sometimes it's not what you say but how you say it, and therefore, how it is perceived.
- Be generous with others who hope to achieve what you have achieved. Each one teach one.
- Be diligent about building and maintaining your personal brand promises.

Exercise – Your Platform

So just exactly what are you an expert in? What is your expertise? How do you want people to recognize you? And how do they find you and your sage advice?

Start with where you are now. Ask a few friends, "What do you think is my area of expertise?" Their answers will be more accurate than your own because you want to know how your public perceives you, not how you perceive yourself.

Once you're done with that, go ahead and jot down a direction you would like to take your platform. Maybe you want to broaden your knowledge of services you can supply to clients (Example: you have expertise in medical/navigational advocacy but you'd like to become more adept and known for shared decision making.) Or maybe you'd like your platform to be a larger reach, like becoming a columnist in your daily paper (or probably more like the online version of your daily paper) which is a broader outreach than just your own website. Becoming a resource for your local media is a great approach as well.

The more varied and extensive your platform, the higher the regard for your authority. So don't limit your platform. Just when you think you've defined it well, add something else. Challenge yourself!

Having determined a good sense of where your perceived authority is today, and where you would like it to go in the future, it's time to extend your reach. The following suggestions are focused on sharing your expertise, because that's how you build expertness – you share it.

There is much more information about many of these ideas in other parts of this book.

- Messages about your expertise (creating expertness and authority):
- Craft messages that are clear and concise
- Share messages in terms your audiences can understand
- Include calls to action
- Share commentary on current events
- Don't be afraid to step on opinion toes as long as you can back up what you say
- Don't be afraid to admit you don't know something, but always follow up and provide additional information later

Tools for sharing:

- Be available for all opportunities (media inquiries, speaking engagements)
- Reach out to media to share your messages (your own PR, or hire a service)
- Create your own opportunities to teach, write or speak on your topic
- Go online! (blog, comment, build your own site)
- Write a book (even an e-book)
- Speak to groups of people whenever you have the opportunity

Exercise – Your Public and Your Pond

Who already follows you, or is interested in what you have to say? And where are they located?

Within the ranks of your followers will be the people you begin to garner income from, either because they pay to hear you speak, or they pay for your advocacy services, or buy a book from you, or in some other way.

We want to know who they are, especially if they are located in your pond.

Start with a list of everyone you know who, if you were so inclined, you might call on the phone to talk about your expertise. (No, I'm not going to ask you to do that, I just want you to figure out who they are.) Remember, these are people who might eventually look to your expertise as something they are willing to pay for. Family, friends, co-workers, other professionals you know like your tax guy or a lawyer. You might know them from work, or your neighborhood, or a club you belong to.

If they are located elsewhere (your parents, siblings and college roommate) then don't toss them off your list, but know they aren't really part of your professional public.

But now, at least, you have a start on the right public who lives in your professional pond. When I started, I had, maybe, 10 people on my list – so don't worry if there aren't many! As of Fall 2014, my 10 people have grown to almost 20,000 email addresses for just my patient empowerment and advocacy work. In such a small pond, that's pretty good. You'll be able to do that too.

▼

Of course, now your goal is to grow your follower list—your public in your pond. Here are some ways you can do that. More thorough descriptions of each of these tactics are covered in other chapters of this book, and in the *Basic Marketing Handbook*.

Gather names and contact information (usually an email address) in every way you can. The way to build your list of followers is to maintain regular contact with them which you will do through outreach like email newsletters or tips, or even direct postal mail. (See Chapter Eleven.) Keep in mind that each of the ideas below requires you add a piece that will allow for collection of names and email addresses.

- ★ ★ ★ Start a blog. Yes – that's three stars, because if I had to give you just one piece of advice about how to establish yourself as an expert, I would tell you to start a blog. I would go so far as to say that if it weren't for blogging, you might have no idea about patient advocacy as a profession or these books as assistance for building your practice.

  That's because I launched my first blog, called Every Patient's Advocate, in 2005. I now have three blogs I write on a regular basis (some more frequently than others). I have written, literally, more than 2000 blog posts over time, and each one has brought me at least one more follower and often more. Find more information about starting and building your blog in Chapter Nine.

- Build your practice website to include a page that is just about you and your expertise. In fact, you may want to make this separate from your business website. I have an EveryPatientsAdvocate.com website and my TrishaTorrey.com (blog) site as well. Both encourage visitors to sign up for an email newsletter. (Chapter Eight)

- Set up your social networking to promote your blog posts and articles, which will encourage people to go to your blog or site to reach them where they will see an opportunity to opt-in to your regular outreach to them. (Chapter Ten.)

- Connect with your local media (or national, if that's your pond), and be a useful resource for commenting on issues that regard your expertise. A thorough discussion of how to do this can be found in the *Basic Marketing Handbook*.

- Look for speaking opportunities (see more in Chapter Seven.) At each one you'll have opportunities to collect contact information for attendees.

- Write a book or e-book, or many of them, and set up a system so that when someone buys them, they can get a free download, and you can collect their email addresses.

- Look for health fairs or senior fairs, church bazaars, or other opportunities where you can set up a table or booth, talk to people who attend, give them a freebie (a pen or tablet) and ask for their contact information in return.

So now we've covered the entire four-legged stool for becoming a recognized expert: your platform, your profile, your pond and your public. You have a snapshot of your expertness status, and some directions to take to grow your authority.

Go for it! It may not be easy to toot your own horn as you get started, but I promise you, it WILL get easier and soon it will just be part of who you are.

If this helps, a few years ago, when my first book was published (a very thrilling occasion!) my husband gave me a decorative tile which I keep near my desk. It says,

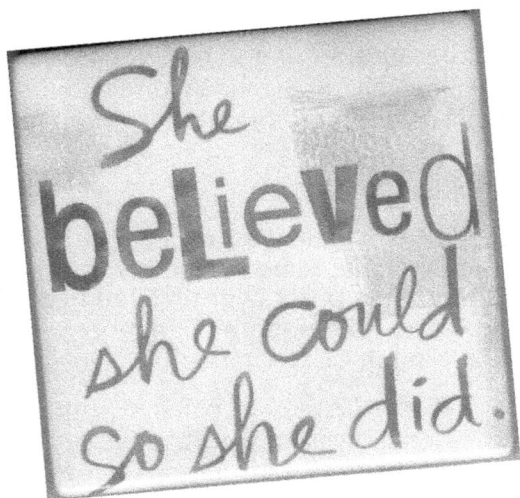

I hope it provides you with a bit of motivation too.

Chapter Five

Strategy: Expanding Your Target Audiences

Josie and Joe, age 12, live next door to each other and have always been best friends. They live in a quiet suburban neighborhood, around the end of a cul-de-sac. Summer vacations stretch long and Josie and Joe are always looking for something to keep themselves busy.

Three years ago when Joe and Josie were 9, they set up a lemonade stand on a hot, sunny July day. They charged 25 cents for a paper cup full of lemonade and a few hours, and batches, and spilled cups, and bullying kids on bikes, and almost-sunburned later, they had sold about $8 worth of lemonade, translating to about $2.80 in profits.

Was it worth their effort? Maybe.

The next year they got a little smarter. Joe asked his mother if they could move their lemonade stand into the back of her mini-SUV. His idea was to take his lemonade stand on the road and not just satisfy people's thirst, but maybe help them, too.

You see, Joe had an uncle with an alcohol problem. One day Joe had asked his uncle why he drank so much. "Because I'm thirsty!" his uncle had replied. So, Joe, in his 10-year-old wisdom which he had developed from asking the entire universe of people he knew with alcohol problems (his uncle) had reasoned that if people who went to bars to drink alcohol did so because they were thirsty, then he could sell them lemonade to drink instead. A better choice for those bar visitors, and money in Joe and Josie's pockets!

As you can imagine, Joe's great idea didn't work out too well. In fact, his mother did take Joe and Josie to set up their lemonade stand on the sidewalk in front of the bar. Most of the people who walked by were polite. A few bought lemonade – but then walked into the bar anyway. Many of the people laughed at Joe and Josie and said things to them like, "Oh, you're so cute!" (which both Joe and Josie found to be condescending.) The bottom line was that they didn't even sell $8 worth of lemonade in front of the bar, plus they were frustrated at their lack of accomplishment.

Was it worth their effort? No, certainly not. Both Joe and Josie felt like failures without even understanding why they had failed.

Then last year, with a couple of years' worth of lemonade stand experience behind them, Josie discussed their lemonade stand with her mother. Her mother gave her very sage advice. "You two need to sell your lemonade where people are very thirsty, don't have many options for quenching that thirst, and have money in their pockets to spend to take care of that discomfort. Wherever they are – that's where you should sell your lemonade."

That made real sense to Josie, so shared her mother's advice with Joe. They asked themselves, who and where are those very thirsty people who don't really have other options for satisfying their thirst? Over the next few days they came up with a great list: construction people working outdoors in the heat (like roofers and road pavers), older kids who went to ball practice or marching band rehearsals, parents hanging out at the park, watching their kids on the playground equipment, and others. Real people who had money in their pockets who would be very happy to find a way to quench their thirst.

And so they were. Last summer Josie and Joe made a small fortune selling lemonade. They had figured out the keys to success: finding the right people, those who could afford to pay them and had a need that could be satisfied with lemonade, provided at the very moment they felt they most needed that lemonade.

Did they rest on their laurels? No, not at all. This year's plans include expanding their reach. A few of their friends want "in" on the lemonade business, so Joe and Josie will teach them the ropes so they can actually reach more customers at more construction sites, and more parks (paying Joe and Josie a piece of the action.) Plus, they are beginning to think about a new way to offer their services by connecting with a new target audience – a new niche. They are going to engage with a few real estate agents to set up their lemonade stand during Open Houses as a way to lure in potential homebuyers.

The future of J&J Thirst Busters is bright!

As most businesses do, it took Joe and Josie a few years to settle into their marketing sweet spot, to develop their markets and then begin to expand their business. They found their real success when they stopped just guessing and crossing their fingers, and made a concerted effort to hone in on specific traits of their target audiences.

....

OK – it's true – lemonade stands are a far cry from health advocacy practices. For one thing, they provide products, not services. Perhaps the biggest difference is a lemonade stand doesn't do much to address life and death or financial security questions for their customers.

Despite the differences, there is much we can learn about target audiences from Joe and Josie's experiences. That's what we will tackle in this chapter.

Primary and Secondary Audiences – Some Differences in Approach

In the *Basic Marketing Handbook*, we learned to assess our target audiences' needs and then present our service offerings to them through their eyes. We learned that understanding and sharing the benefits of our work to them is far more important and effective than listing the services we provide.

We also broke our audiences out into Primary and Secondary, where primary audiences are the people who will hire you and pay you directly, like the elder population, someone who has been diagnosed with something difficult and scary, perhaps life threatening (cancer, ALS), or people who have received hospital or doctor bills that are far too high. Your primary audiences may vary depending on the services you offer.

Secondary audiences are "influencers;" those people who will influence someone else to hire us, although eventually they may hire us themselves. An adult child of an elderly parent; a pastor, priest or rabbi who might know that someone in their parish or temple could use your help; your local radio station's top talk show personality who might interview you and open the ears and eyes of someone who could use your services - we'll look more closely at secondary audiences later in this chapter.

Primary Audiences – Who Is the Right Client?

Early in your advocacy practice, if someone asked you who, as a professional patient advocate, you could help, you might have said, "Everyone who needs help with the healthcare system."

And yes – maybe you COULD help all those people.

Or, maybe you have whittled it down some to develop a niche, choosing to work only with cancer patients, or the elderly, or surgery patients, or ? We tackled the primary audience determination quite well in the *Basic Marketing HandBook*, and niches in Chapter Three, earlier in this book.

Instead we are going to tighten our definition of primary audiences in this *Advanced Marketing Handbook*. That is, that even having defined your primary target audiences perfectly, there is probably one attribute about them you have missed.

The problem is that, as a business owner, there are some people even within the target audiences you have defined that you CAN'T or SHOULDN'T try to help – not because you don't know how to, or don't have the skills. Rather, because they don't fit the criteria for the RIGHT client:

Criteria - the Right Primary Client

1. ... has (or had) a medical challenge. (Or, their loved one has or had a medical challenge. For purposes of this discussion, we include loved ones, too.)

2. ... that challenge has had a negative impact on her life which may continue to be problematic to her for the long term. We call it FUDGE: fear, uncertainty, doubt, guilt and/or exhaustion. The right client exhibits some combination of those emotions.

3. ... recognizes that he or she needs help to overcome or remove that negativity.

4. ... recognizes that the services YOU offer have the potential to allay that negativity.

5. ... has the ability and willingness to pay you, and recognizes that the value he or she will receive from working with you is worth what you charge.

Identification of the right primary target audience client means they will meet all five criteria. **Unless a potential client exhibits all five attributes, they will not hire you.**

I'm sure you are nodding your head right now. This makes sense when spelled out like this, right? It makes so much sense that you almost have to wonder why we would bother wasting marketing book space on the subject...

Here's why: because too often private advocates go in search of anyone who fits attributes 1-4, without much regard to 5. But #5 is so important, that it might belong first on the list!

As obvious as this point about being willing and able to pay is, most advocates don't keep it in mind when they develop their marketing. Here are some examples.

Here are marketing tactics that real advocates have used. Which makes more sense?

1. Running an ad in your daily newspaper that reaches a general population of 200,000 people for $500?   or   Running an ad in a weekly newspaper that is sold only in a high-income suburb that reaches a population of 30,000 for $400?

2. Speaking for one hour to a large group of older people as they eat their free lunch in a senior center, then staying afterward to enjoy dessert with them?   or   Speaking for one hour to a 12-member Rotary Club during their luncheon meeting, then buying your own lunch afterward?

You may already know the answers after our discussion of being sure people can pay you, but here they are just in case:

- In the first example, the obvious answer is that the people in the high-wealth suburb are more likely to have the ability to pay you.

- In the second example, the answer is that older people attending free lunch sessions at the local senior center may truly need your help, but most of them will never satisfy that #5 requirement. There is a better chance you'll be hired by a Rotarian who might have a health challenge himself, or an elderly parent who could use your help.

We're not going to spend more time with primary audiences here. Refer to the *Basic Marketing Handbook* for a thorough review of marketing to primary audiences, then pair those lessons with what you learned in Chapter Three of this advanced book about market niches. The new addition to the mix, of course, is their ability to pay.

Instead we're going to look at tapping into secondary audiences and their reach.

The Importance of Secondary Target Audiences - a Shortcut to Success?

Everyone loves a shortcut if it means more success for less work, money or effort, right?

If that's true for you, then marketing to secondary audiences might fit the bill.

A secondary target audience (STA); is usually not the person who will pay you directly for your work, nor the person you actually advocate for. Rather, they will influence someone else to hire you and pay you for the work you do.[10]

An STA is someone who is held in enough esteem by the person who will hire you and pay you that their suggestion will be taken very seriously, and possibly acted on.

An STA might be the adult child of elderly parents who need assistance. The adult child convinces Dad to hire you as his advocate (of course, it's possible the adult child will hire you directly, even though Dad will be the client you work with.)

Sometimes, if you market very well, you can eventually turn someone who is an STA into a primary target audience. In effect, they begin as a referral source, then turn out to be your client – nice shortcut, right?

Examples:

- An employer (STA) might promote your services to her employees (eventually becoming a primary audience when she hires you and pays you to work with her employees.)

- Some large churches (STA) have nurses on staff, and those nurses can be hired independently by parishioners. If nurses, why not advocates?

---

10 In the *Basic Marketing Handbook*, we called them Influencers. For our purposes here, Secondary Target Audiences and Influencers are mostly interchangeable.

- Or – my own marketing story is a perfect example of turning an STA into a primary audience. That is, that when I began my patient empowerment work, my primary target audience was patients and caregivers – those people who would pay me to speak or buy my books or read my articles online. But it soon became apparent that I could never reach out to as many individuals as I wanted to – not just little old me! It also became apparent that if I supported ONE ADVOCATE (my STA), then that one advocate could eventually help HUNDREDS OF PATIENTS.... To the point where advocates are now, in practice, my primary target audience, reaching my original primary audience every day.

As a private advocate, that's how your audiences can work, too, especially if your intent is to grow your practice.

- For example, say you decide employers will be a secondary audience. You begin your outreach to them, they refer you to some of their employees who pay you privately for your work for them.

- Your work is so successful that the employer sees how useful it can be to her; employees who have worked with you have missed work less frequently, her employer-supplied healthcare costs are going down...

- So she asks you whether she can hire you to work for more employees (perhaps the ones who are lower paid and can't afford your services themselves, or maybe the expensive employees in the C-suite because when they miss work for illness it's terribly expensive to the enterprise!) You agree, and bring two more professionals into your practice because your workload is too large with so many folks to help.

- Then the employer asks you if you would be interested in speaking to a local networking group she belongs to, comprised of small business CEOs and human resource professionals. You agree, you speak, and the next thing you know, more businesses want to contract with your company to supply services to their employees...

Eventually you may reach a point where you need to make a decision about whether you want to continue working with one client at a time who calls you because he found you on the web, or whether you'll want to refocus all your marketing toward those STAs who have now become your primary audiences.

So now you see why focusing on secondary audiences can be a shortcut to success.

Criteria - the Right Secondary Target Audience Member

Just like we listed criteria for our primary audiences, let's also list some for STAs.

Your STA:

- ... has a clear wish to help someone who is having difficulty with their journey through the healthcare system.

- ... recognizes that the services you offer have the potential to provide an improved experience for that person.

- ... is willing to recommend you and your services to that person they hope to help.

- ... understands that there are costs and fees for your services and won't make the recommendation unless they are (relatively) certain that person will be willing and able to pay you for your work.

If you compare them side-by-side, you'll see that these criteria are not exactly the same as those we listed for primary audiences. One of the biggest differences is in the question of understanding and willingness to pay for services.

For primary audiences, it will be up to you to make sure they understand this attribute, and you will have to determine yourself whether they meet that criterion.

But for secondary audiences, you will have to rely on someone else's assessment of the clients' ability and willingness to pay.

Who Are They, these Secondary Target Audiences?

I'm not going to keep you guessing. Instead I'm going to provide you with a starter list of potential secondary audiences you might want to tap into. Then we're going to look at what makes them good STAs and what you'll need to do to market to them.

Important: Not every group on this list is a good STA for YOUR practice. These are just suggestions, groups to consider. Don't try to reach out to them until you've worked on the next part of this chapter, *How to Market to Secondary Target Audiences*.

For each of these groups, I've listed the audience, and supporting information. More information and resources can be found in the ORB. ORB

- **Employers**
  Every employer wants to save money on healthcare and support their employees as well. Their overall healthcare costs can be reduced and managed when someone assists their employees and teaches them to be more responsible patients. Both absenteeism and presenteeism[11] can be reduced by providing access to an advocate which also lowers the employer's expenses. You may be able to get employers to pay you for providing services to their employees (for example, their EAP, Employee Assistance Program) or they may allow you to include information in their employee newsletter in return for "discounting" the price of your services to their employees – or anything in between.

---

11 Presenteeism = when someone is at work, and being paid, but is spending time making phone calls or accessing the Internet for personal reasons instead of doing the work s/he is paid for.

- **Unions**
  In recent years, unions have struggled to survive in a difficult labor climate. They are looking for relevance in the form of new benefits for their members and their families; benefits that will not only improve their lives, but will be important enough to them that they will continue to pay union dues. You might negotiate discounted pricing for union members if the union invites you to set up a table during meetings, or allows you to write articles for their newsletter, or in some way helps you market your services to their entire membership.

- **Attorneys**
  A number of legal specialties intersect with advocacy. In particular those who deal with eldercare, trust and estate work, personal injury, malpractice, workers comp and other law that pertains to individuals and their health. You can become a new revenue stream for an attorney who can sell your services to his or her clients.

  Attorneys may also be considered as strategic partners. See page 55 for more about strategic partners.

- **Financial Planners**
  The one thing financial planners want more of is client money that can be invested in the products a financial planner sells. Even fee-for-service financial planners (who are not paid by commission, but instead are paid by the hour for the advice they give) recognize that their clients' abilities to invest will be affected by the cost of healthcare not just today but into their future, especially during their retirement. To the extent you can help their clients save money, either by helping them navigate the healthcare system more efficiently, or by reviewing their medical bills and negotiating them down, financial planners will love to recommend that their clients work with you.

- **Senior Moving Specialists**
  When older folks downsize or move into senior apartments, retirement centers, assisted living, skilled nursing centers, or CCRCs (Continuing Care Retirement Communities) they can use all the help they can get. Often their adult children live elsewhere, but even if they are only an hour or two away it's still not an easy task to get Mom, Dad or both moved. Senior Moving Specialists to the rescue! Often older adults who must move do so because they have health challenges, and therefore, having someone like you to recommend to the senior or the family is a nice feather in a Senior Moving Specialist's cap.

- **Real Estate Agents**
  Similar to Senior Moving Specialists, real estate agents may also be working with people who have health challenges. There is little chance they will hire you themselves, but when they can make referrals to someone like you at the right time, they become heroes, improving the chances they will be hired again themselves.

- **Churches / Synagogues / Temples**
  These religious may help identify those people who could use your help and can afford it too.

- **Physicians** (some) I've put physicians toward the end of this list because they are a tough sell. They may be willing to refer you as a pass-through (handing a patient your brochure, for example) but their insurance reimbursements don't usually leave room to pay you themselves.

  Direct pay physicians (also called concierge or boutique practices), those who do not accept health insurance, may be more likely to consider referring you to their patients and/or eventually hiring you themselves. If you can demonstrate that being available to their patients can save the doctor money on the delivery of care, s/he might be interested in a long term contract with you.

- **Hospitals** – Beginning in 2012, Medicare began to penalize hospitals for patients who were discharged, but later returned to the hospital within 30 days. Therefore, some hospitals might consider hiring private advocates for post discharge monitoring or other services that will help keep them out of the penalty box. A hospital's decision-maker will be a chief financial officer who may not even realize (or care about) the health benefits to their patients; who instead will be more interested in how you save them money.

Strategic Partners as STAs

In addition to the potential STAs listed above different group of people all together: Strategic Partners.

What differentiates a strategic partner from the rest of the STAs is simply that a strategic partner is already in business doing something complimentary to your work, but by combining your talents and services you expand business for both of you.

For example, you might find that partnering (strategically!) with another advocate allows you to expand your services. You are a navigator, your potential partner is a billing and claims specialist. By forming a partnership, you can both work with one client and maximize the services provided and the income earned.

The goal in working with a strategic partner is to compliment and enhance each other's work. It's not simply a referral (which is what most of the STAs are). Rather, it's a cooperative venture.

Other professions that could be considered strategic partners are other advocates whose services are complimentary to yours, geriatric care managers, case or care managers, guardians and conservators, health coaches, attorneys, and life care planners (who most often work for, and are paid by attorneys, for creating management plans for people who have become disabled.) You can find more resources for each of these groups in the ORB.

Get Started: Marketing to Secondary Target Audiences

On previous pages, I've provided a brief overview of the interests in your work of each of the STAs and strategic partners.

Using that information, and your own knowledge of these audiences, It's time for you to create two charts:

The first one is a **Macro Audience Chart** – a review of audiences, their needs, and your possibilities of success in general. The Macro Chart will steer you in the right direction for your choice of specific individuals or companies, and then, it will frame your marketing.

The second one will be your **Micro Audience Chart**. Once you've completed the Macro Chart, you'll be able to choose the one or two secondary audiences or strategic partners you want to begin focusing on. Those choices will help you populate the Micro Audience Chart with specific companies or individuals to begin marketing your services to, based on the answers you determine as you put it together.

Exercise – Your STA Macro Audience Chart

With either pencil and paper, or in an electronic spreadsheet (like Excel) or a table in a word processed document, draw a table with 6 columns and 12 rows.

Across the top, put these questions, one above each column.

- Column 1: Name of the STA (employers, unions, etc)

- Column 2: Why would they recommend you to someone else? (WIIFM? - see page 57*)

- Column 3: Why might they eventually hire you themselves? (WIIFM? - see page 57*)

- Column 4: What's in it for the people (patients) they would recommend you to?* (WIIFM? - see page 57*)

- Column 5: Additional Notes (for whatever you think of you'd like to add)

- Column 6: (Then leave the last column blank for now.)

Skip a row, then add one STA (as listed on page 53) per row. If you know you have no interest in reaching out to one of the listed audiences, just skip it. Yes, there will be a few extra rows. That's so you can add any additional audiences you think of that aren't listed here.

If you have interest in working with strategic partners, you can add them to this list too.

Now – start filling in all the empty fields. Yes – it's a chore! But as you work on it, you'll begin to get some real clarity in the interests of these different audiences and how you might be able to make inroads with the people they may refer you to.

* Columns 2, 3 and 4: WIIFM?

This is the real core, the meat of why these different groups are good STAs. The key is the answer to WIIFM? What's In It for Me? Remember, being hired by them is all about making the benefits to working with you very clear. If they asked you, "WIIFM?" how would you answer them? They don't care about your services except as your services help THEM. That's true no matter whether they are primary or secondary audiences.

For example: Why would an employer recommend you? Because you can help an employee navigate the healthcare system? No! Not really! Yes, they want their employees to be happy and feel supported, but you need to think how to answer their question, WIIFM?

One reason it makes sense for an employer to recommend you (and eventually hire you) is because working with you can cut down on rates of absenteeism. (Keep in mind, employees might be absent not just when they are sick themselves, but also when a family member is sick.) Working with you can also cut down on rates of presenteeism. Working with you can help save them money when patients choose less expensive treatments (Because, of course, they pay part of the employees' insurance premiums.) You may think of additional reasons.

Another example: Why would a union recommend you? Or hire you? Why is it a benefit to them to make their members aware you can help them? Or to hire you to serve their members? If the union boss asked you WIIFM? - how would you answer? One reason is because they are losing the battle to stay relevant in today's society (although we never know when that can change). As a result, they are on the lookout for benefits to provide members to keep members from leaving their union. Further, even though the union negotiates pay and benefits with employers, their members (like everyone else) are paying a bigger slice of the health insurance premium pie, and may be looking for help to determine ways to save money with their healthcare, or to review their medical bills, or whatever services you might offer. (Of course, strong labor unions aren't found in all corners of the country, so this may not be a STA that would work well for you.)

Once you have completed your STA Macro Chart, you will have a good idea of what audiences seem interesting to you, which of those audiences you want to pursue, and how you can help them. You'll even have a good start on your messaging.

Which takes us to the last column. Look over your audiences, and prioritize them. The one you are most interested in approaching is #1, next is #2 and so forth.

▼

Now it's time for your first Micro Audience Chart. Yes, I said first – because you could end up with as many Micro Audience Charts as there are audiences. But for right now we're going to develop only one, and we're going to use the STA you chose as your #1 priority in you STA Macro Audience Chart.

EXERCISE – Your First Micro Audience Chart

Similarly to your STA Macro Chart, with either pencil and paper, or in an electronic spreadsheet (like Excel) or a word processed document, draw a table with 5 columns and 12 rows.

Leave the tops of the columns blank for the moment, skip down two (blank) rows, and write in the following questions / details:

Row 1: Decision Maker (this is the person who will ultimately decide whether or not they or their organization will be willing to work with you to make referrals or even hire you. Even if this person isn't the CEO or COO of the company, this person will be THE most important person to you.)

- Row 2: phone

- Row 3: email

Row 4: Other important personnel

- Row 5: phone

- Row 6: email

Row 7: Your Own Affiliation (meaning – who do you know who is connected to this organization and could make an introduction)

- Row 8: phone

- Row 9: email

Row 10: Likeliness of Needing the Help You Can Provide (Rate this on a scale of 1-5 with 1 representing a large likelihood you can help them. This will be just your guesstimate based on what you know about the organization. For example, think about employers – an ad agency is generally staffed by a younger group of employees. If your niche is cancer navigation, then it might not be a good audience. But if you choose instead a manufacturing company where many employees do all-day manual labor, and your niche is orthopedic navigation, there could be a host of reasons they could need your services.)

Row 11: Additional Notes

Row 12: leave this one blank for now

You've probably guessed what happens next. Yes, you're going to work on your #1 priority STA by coming up with the names of 3-5 real businesses, organizations, or people who would fall under that STA, who you will potentially contact to discuss working with them.

Examples: Say you decide Financial Planners are a perfect audience for your services. You love to help people in that 55-65 age group, many of whom are trying to save every penny they can for their retirement, but may face some expensive health challenges. So let's fill in your chart. You might start with your own Planner. In the second column of your chart, write that person's name.

Or, maybe you think a good group to begin with would be employers. Choose a business that has enough people so you know the employer offers health insurance coverage. Maybe you know of personnel from such businesses through a networking group you participate with, or the Chamber of Commerce. Maybe your spouse or partner works for a company you think would be a good target.

Now go ahead and fill out your chart. For some choices of businesses or people, you won't need all fields. In some cases you'll need to go online or make a phone call for information like phone numbers or email addresses.

You may not be able to get all the answers you need right away. Sometimes the toughest answer to discern is just who the decision maker will be – and to you, that information is gold. Because that is the most important person you will talk to in that organization.

Go ahead and fill in as much information as you can for your 3-5 choices. Finally, on line 12, go ahead and prioritize the organizations you've explored.

A lot of work, right? Well, nobody ever said marketing is easy! But you have actually just completed most of the hard part, and you're ready for your next steps.

Your next steps are tasks you've done before, assuming (yes, I know what they say) you have read through and worked on the tasks in *The Health Advocate's Basic Marketing Handbook*.

It is time now for you to begin developing your messages for this one business, organization or person from your secondary target audience who you have chosen to reach out to – your priority #1.

You already have a head start, because you've answered the basics of "what's in it for me?" for the entire STA. But now you'll have the opportunity to create even more concise messages.

Do your first outreach by phone, email or postal mail to your affiliation (friend) or the decision-maker. You may then be invited to meet with them to discuss your ideas further, or to put together a proposal.

During that exchange, your primary job is to LISTEN LISTEN LISTEN (even if you are just reading an email – pay attention!) because they will tell you about the problems they have, or the solutions they need. They won't give away too much information, and you may have to listen between the words they use (listen for unspoken hurdles they have encountered) but eventually you will get information from them that will help you tailor your messages very specifically to their needs. That's when you can take the messages you have already crafted, and refine them to be very specific to that person, business or organization.

We are not going to deal with the specifics of a proposal here—there are just too many variables—except to say that the more they see exactly what they need, and potential solutions to the problems they are having, the better your chances of scoring some business from them.

Two more points to make.

First, you won't be able to make inroads with every person, organization or business you list on your Micro Charts. In fact, a good rule of thumb is that you may be invited to meet with maybe one out of five you even approach - 20%. Expect to hear at least 4 "nos" for every "yes" you hear.

If you've attempted meetings with (what you consider to be) too many representatives of the STA you chose as your #1 priority, and you aren't making inroads, the you can do a few things:

You may want to look at refining your messages, or at asking more specific questions about their challenges so you can tailor your information more accurately. You may want to try a different STA which might produce a better success rate. Or, you can just keep trying! The winners, the successes, are the people who know that you have to kiss a lot of target audience frogs, both primary and secondary, to build a business.

We've now covered four new marketing strategies you can take advantage of: expanding your brand, developing your niche, becoming a recognized expert, and expanding your reach to new target audiences, both secondary audiences and strategic partners.

They are great ideas for growing your practice! But the real proof will be in their execution.

So let's begin to look at some of these advanced marketing tactics.

Chapter Six

Tactic: Customer (Client) Service

This tactic will:

- Create trust among your audiences
- Drive audiences to other marketing information
- Establish your authority
- Support all other aspects of your marketing

When asked what they think "customer service" is, or means, most people reply with something like "fixing a problem," or "giving me a refund," or "the customer is always right."

To me, those are simply ways customer service can be executed, but they aren't really what customer service is ABOUT.

To me, customer service describes every encounter you have with an individual, before, during, and after your direct work with them. For our private advocacy purposes, we need to call it "client service" perhaps. But the point is, that every word you speak (or don't speak), every activity you undertake on their behalf, every solution you provide, and every follow up you offer, those interfaces are part of your customer – or client service.

Some of the most powerful marketing you will execute will be everyday client service. And when you consider the price is right (your time only) then you understand why client service as a marketing tactic needs to be right at the top of the list.

Why do I consider client service to be marketing?

Because when it's done well, it sells your services like nothing else can. Good client service provides positive word-of-mouth, the most powerful marketing that exists. It's putting your action where your mouth is. It's practicing what you preach.

Good customer service creates trust, loyalty, devotion, and more business, not just from that one client, but from the additional people he or she tells about you.

On the other hand, bad client service, or even just substandard client service, provides the most powerful anti-marketing – a reason for someone to decide NOT to work with you. Poor client service causes you to lose clients directly, and can elicit word-of-mouth that is so negative that future potential clients will run in the other direction.

The Proof Is in the Stats

You don't need to simply take my word for it that good customer service has an impact on business. An interesting article called *50 Facts about Customer Experience* cites studies done by the US Chamber of Commerce, the White House Office of Consumer Affairs, and other large organizations. They include the following:

On the positive side:

- Loyal customers are worth up to ten times as much as their first purchase.
- The probability of selling to a new customer is 5-20 percent, while selling to an existing customer is 60-70 percent.

And on the negative side:

- It takes 12 positive experiences to make up for a single bad experience.
- 78 percent of consumers have ended a transaction due to bad service.
- For every customer who complains, 26 others don't speak up.
- Negative interactions with a business are spread to twice as many people as positive ones.

Clearly, as business owners, our goals need to be about attending to the positive outcomes, and avoiding the negatives.

The Basic Tenets of an Advocate's Client Service

Like many other topics in this book, customer or client service could be its own book. If you do an online search for books about customer service, you'll find there are dozens. But I've attempted a client service boot camp for you here.

And – to manage your expectations – this is client service, one-on-one with a client. This isn't about working with your influencer audiences, although many of the tenets I've spelled out could probably be applied to them too.

Whether you already provide good client service, or you aren't sure whether you do or do not, here are the basics you need to embrace to provide both you and your client with satisfaction that your relationship is all it can be:

• Treat Your (Potential) Clients Like Heroes

If you approach each one as if he or she deserves to be put on a platform, you'll get a good sense of how you should speak to them and behave around them. Now, I'm not saying you need to genuflect, or call them "madam" or "sir." What I am saying is that small touches help them understand their importance to you – and that regard will be reciprocated.

Examples:

- Ask them what they would like to be called (first names? Mrs. or Mr.?)
- Be sure you always spell their names correctly.
- Take time with them as if they are your ONLY client – although you can also manage their expectations about time too (see more in this section.)
- Let them hear you credit others instead of yourself – it will make them feel like part of a team.

• Never Reject A Request Out of Hand

Well – at least don't dismiss an idea without providing an alternative.

Of course, there will be times a client asks us to do something we can't or shouldn't do for them. Perhaps they ask you to review a medical bill – but that's not in your skill set. Or they ask you to tell them how to handle a medical decision, and ask you what you would do. By contract you can't give them an answer.

But don't just say, "Sorry, I can't." or "No, I don't do that work."

Instead, try to provide an alternative. Offer to introduce your client to a colleague or strategic partner who can help them. If a client insists you make a decision for her, politely reiterate your contractual agreements, but offer to try to list pros and cons.

The key is not to create a stone wall over which one of you will need to climb. Instead, create bridges so that a potential chasm can be more easily crossed.

• Ask, then Listen

One of the biggest complaints I hear from patients, caregivers and other clients is that they feel as if they aren't being heard. I suspect you could tell me stories of clients who are frustrated that their doctors and providers don't listen – what a loud clue that listening is what they need from you!

Don't ever assume that you know what someone feels, or thinks, or has to say. Don't ever assume you know what their opinions or preferences are. Even if you think you know, even if you are quite clear, you can't be sure, and you need to go to the source – your client.

Everyone likes to be asked. And in general I think most advocates are good about asking.

But the second part is vital: Listen carefully! This is what will separate you from providers, and your advocacy competition. The advocate who truly listens, and embraces answers, and acts accordingly, will be the one whose practice will flourish.

Ask. Listen. Then ask more questions if you need to. Repeat back what you've been told to be sure you are clear. Double check that the two of you understand words in the same way.

Clear communication means you are both on the same wavelength, and that is required for great client service, and great outcomes.

Examples:

Ask for clear times a client prefers to be contacted. For example, some people aren't morning people, so if you usually call at 9 AM, that might not be the best time for them. They won't necessarily tell you that! But they'll feel great that you asked.

If they want to complain about something or someone, listen for a few minutes, then ask them what their preference would have been. From there see if you can segue into finding a better solution based on those preferences.

• Manage Expectations

If you've read any of my books, you know this is my mantra! I swear, being able to effectively and consistently manage expectations could solve the ALL the world's problems. (Of course, that might then mean that no one would need a patient advocate? Ah... but then, I digress.)

Managing expectations is the most effective way there is to communicate clearly and to be sure you and your client understand the same things.

That's true whether you are talking about something positive or negative. Here's an example I use often in a healthcare environment:

> Delores has a 10 AM appointment with her doctor. She arrives at 9:55, gets checked in, and is sent to the waiting room. At 10:30 she's still waiting, so she asks the receptionist if there is a problem - Delores thinks she has been forgotten. The snippy receptionist tells her they are obviously running behind but will get to her as soon as they can. Finally, at 10:45, Delores is called back to the exam room.

> Delores isn't happy, and is even more annoyed because the receptionist was so snippy. She complains to her doctor, then her doctor is on edge, and the rest of the appointment goes badly because nobody is happy.

Contrast that with this story:

> Delores has a 10 AM appointment with her doctor. She arrives at 9:55, and while checking in, the receptionist tells her the doctor is running behind due to an early morning emergency. Delores is given the option – she can wait for what might be up to an extra hour, or she can reschedule her appointment. Delores decides that since she is already there, she might as well wait.

> At 10:45 she gets called to the exam room. Delores is so relieved she didn't have to wait an entire hour! They were ready for her early! She and the doctor have a good discussion. Overall Delores and her doctor are satisfied with the appointment.

In both scenarios, the doctor was running late. In both, Delores had to wait the same amount of time. But the outcome of the second is so much more positive than the first....

The only difference? In the second scenario, Delores' expectations were managed.

In every step of your work with your client, explain exactly what the client can expect, and when, and what you will do if somehow things don't go as planned. (See Plan B on page 66.) Even negative news is much easier to handle when it's not unexpected.

• Be Professionally Empathetic

When asked, many patients today will tell you that it seems like no one in healthcare cares about their well-being anymore. What they have identified is a lack of empathy. Too many doctors skip over the "how are you?" question, or cut off the answer too quickly. Patients have noticed, they miss it, and they don't like it.

Which is why it's a primary touch point where advocates can make a huge difference, and be appreciated by their clients. A few "I'm so sorry to hear that's" and "I can't even imagine how much that must hurt's" can go a long way toward your positive relationship with your client.

It's important that you care, and that you act like you care. On the other hand, there is a thin line between empathy and caring too much. I wish I could tell you exactly where that line is, but I can't. What I can tell you is some symptoms of where you are getting close or have crossed it:

- If you find yourself doing work for your client, but you aren't charging for the time.
- If you find yourself spending way too much time on the phone over topics that aren't related to your work.
- If you find yourself driving a client even though you aren't insured to do so....

Those kinds of things.

The problem is, and the reason this point shows up under Client Service, is that not only won't your work be appreciated as it should be, but that these kinds of space violations are the very things that create client service problems. You know what they say, that 'no good deed goes unpunished."

Don't put yourself in that position. Keep the professional boundaries. Your client will actually have more respect for you in the long run and won't work so hard to take advantage of your good graces.

• Use the Manners Yer Momma Tawcha

This should go without saying, except that sometimes within customer service, Momma missed the boat.

I'm going to teach you two things my dad actually taught me. I have passed these on numerous times, and yet I'm always floored that people never think of them.

1. Never assume someone recognizes your voice when you call them on the phone. If you just launch into the call, or say simply, "It's me," then they may be three

sentences behind by the time they figure out who you are. It's potentially embarrassing, plus it will take longer to regroup and get caught up. Even if you are quite sure they MUST know your voice, begin your conversation by saying who you are. "Hi Mrs. Kenwood. This is Frank."

2. When you see someone in person for the first time in a while, or in a place that you don't usually see them, don't ask, "Do you remember me?" How embarrassing if they can't place you! Why would you want to embarrass them? And, I guarantee that if you do cause embarrassment, they will not become your client – ever, or if they were previously – again. Instead, use your own name (which also invites them to provide theirs...) "Jack! So good to see you! I'm Frank Henderson... we met last summer at the Johnsons..." Of course, Jack remembers you! (Or at least he does now....)

• Anticipate Your Clients' Needs

There will be many times you client doesn't ask you for something because they either don't know they need it, or they don't know you offer it. Not only is it a great relief to them that you are resourceful, it can be a good way to expand the amount of business you do with them.

Example:

> Adult child Linda lives several states away from Mom who needs to be hospitalized. Linda asks you if you will make arrangements for Mom's transportation, and prepare Mom's home for when she returns to the house. Good client service is a suggestion to Linda that it's a smart move to arrange for your mother to have a bedside companion while she is in the hospital; someone to keep an eye on hand washing to avoid infection, drug dissemination, transfers and so forth.... Keeping an eye on things for safety purposes even more so than just to keep her company. Linda concurs – Mom stays safe, and you've got some new business.

It's true that most of us don't know what we need when we are in a difficult situation. We don't even know the questions to ask.

Clients appreciate when you raise these kinds of suggestions. They'll either jump at them right away, they'll think about them, or they'll dismiss them. In any case, it has given you a chance to talk about your services, framed for them, and to expand your billable hours.

• Take Your Umbrella (Plan B)

You know - if you take your umbrella then it probably won't rain.

You and I both know that too often, the best laid plans fall apart. Which is why, sometimes, you need that umbrella – your Plan B.

The point here is that if you plan ahead with a couple of options, then when something doesn't work the way it should, you don't have to miss a beat to take care of the situation.

Think of how great that approach to customer service is! There's no lag time between being disappointed that something didn't go well, and moving on to the next thing. No one has time to get upset. Your client will think you are a genius, especially if you have managed his expectations ahead of time as to what your Plan B umbrella looks like.

An example:

> Your client is scheduled for chemo on Tuesday afternoon. She has been told her treatment will be finished around 4 PM, so you all agree that her husband will leave work a little early to pick her up and take her home. Not only does that take care of her transportation, it also allows him to hear any departing instructions so both of them know what to expect, and what to do once she gets home.

> But you, oh smart and well-prepared advocate, know that even the most devoted spouses can't always leave work on time. So before your client leaves for her chemo treatment on Tuesday, you take a few things to her to stick in her bag that will provide some peace of mind. Included is a small hand-held recorder so she can record any instructions given to her, plus your phone number so that if her husband can't leave work, and she gets stuck, she can phone you to make other transportation arrangements for her. (Of course, you can actually create an entire gift bag for her – but these are the Plan B items that bring peace of mind.)

• Continually Ask for Feedback

Imagine having a long-term relationship with someone and never providing feedback about how that relationship is going. There could be aspects of the relationship that are just like a stone in your shoe, but if you don't speak up, no one will ever remove that stone.

Make sure your client understands that you want and need feedback on a regular basis so you can be sure you are addressing her needs well. "Mrs. Rodriguez, last time I made the appointment for 10am on a Thursday. Was that a good time and day for you?"

Of major importance is some sort of survey at the conclusion of your work together. There are a handful of applications online (Many are free. Find a list in the ORB) that allow you to put together questions, send a link to the person to be surveyed and then help you translate the answers.

You'll want to know things like:

- Were you satisfied with the service you experienced from XYZ Advocates? (yes/no)
- What did you feel were our greatest strengths? (multiple choice)
- If you could improve one aspect of our work with you, what would it be? (multiple choice)
- Considering the cost of our service, how would you rate the overall value? (multiple choice from worth more than they paid, to not worth what they paid.)
- On a scale of 1 to 5 with 5 being the best, would you recommend XYZ Advocates to a friend or colleague?
- There may be other questions you want to ask too.

You'll get the most responses if you make all the questions easy to answer, with yes/no or multiple choice. You can always provide a box for comments at the end of each question, or the end of the survey.

Also, consider allowing them to answer anonymously to give you a better chance of getting objective input.

This type of survey is highly valuable in its ability to improve your service in the future.

• Stay in Touch

Throughout your relationship with your client, you will likely be in regular contact.

But sometimes advocate-client relationships can last over a period of months, with weeks going by with no contact.

And, of course, the best relationships have a natural end when the patient no longer needs you (hopefully because your excellent work means they don't need the type of assistance you provide any longer.)

If you are in the middle of a project, be sure to stay in regular contact with your client. Touch base at least weekly just to let them know where things stand, even if there has been no progress. Don't let them wonder what's going on. Contacting them lets them know they are on your mind and that you care about the relationship.

If your work has ended with them, then ask if you can put them on your email list, and that will be a good way to stay in regular touch with them without extra effort. But make yourself a note a few months after your work is complete just to call and follow-up – to see how things are going, maybe whether they need to re-engage with you for more work.

Measuring Your Success

One of the differences between marketing strategies and tactics is the ability to measure their success. By measuring the success of your tactics, you can make corrections if necessary.

Measuring client service isn't an exact science like some marketing tactics can be. Overall, if clients stay with you, or re-up on their contracts, then you know it must be going well.

You can also measure your success by welcoming new clients who have been referred to you, and by reviewing the answers to client service surveys your clients fill out.

Most of your measurement of customer service will come from the regular feedback you receive as your work together goes along. Hopefully your clients won't allow stones to stay in their shoes for too long without giving you the chance to remove them.

More likely you'll hear plenty of thank-yous, and appreciation – and even receive plenty of hugs – as your work proceeds. You'll know you're doing something – including client service – right.

Chapter Seven

Tactic:
Public (and Not-So-Public) Speaking

This tactic will:

- Expand your business brand

- Expand your personal brand

- Maximize your reach by teaching more people about advocacy

(Remember those "Choose Your Own Adventure" books written for young kids? This chapter will work like one of those....)

- If public speaking doesn't scare you and all you need is some "how to" information, then skip to the section later in this chapter entitled, "Public Speaking Planning—Making It Happen and Getting It Done" on page 76.

- If, on the other hand, you have any fear or trepidation about public speaking, then just keep reading....

I wish I had a nickel for everyone who has told me how much they dislike public speaking. Some actually shudder when they utter those two words.

No doubt it harkens back to those times in school when we had to stand up and recite something, or give a book report, or read a paper we had written. What we knew was that we were being judged, and that no one in the rest of the room wanted to be there.

It's no wonder public speaking always shows up on the lists of people's biggest fears! In fact, in one study in 2010[12], it was the second worst fear, behind only snakes. For most of us, if we avoid it, what would be the purpose of facing those kinds of fears?

---

12 http://joyfulpublicspeaking.blogspot.com/2010/08/what-do-us-college-students-fear-most.html

If you are working to build any new business then public speaking can be a crucial marketing activity. If you have an active dislike of public speaking, then it is time for you to stare down your fear, and to meet it head on.

So the goal of this chapter is to convince you of two things whether or not you have a fear of public speaking:

1. That public speaking can be an enormous boon to your advocacy marketing – Enormous, as in huge. In fact, early on, your willingness to do so, and the skill you develop to address larger groups, can make your marketing easier, and propel you into success far quicker than any other marketing you do. (Further, sadly, that failure to do so may be the reason you don't succeed.)

2. That public speaking doesn't need to be any more "public" than you want it to be. It doesn't need to be about standing in front of large groups of strangers. It may be, therefore, far less scary than you may think, and simple enough that even you will be willing to give it a try.

Rose Gardens, Cannonballs and Public Speaking

Early in the launch of any business is the need to bring in new customers or clients. No matter how perfectly you have crafted your business plan or your marketing plan, no matter how much money you have in your business bank account, no matter how well organized your office is – none of that matters if you don't have clients who will pay you to do your work.

One of your main marketing strategies will be to expose as many people as possible to the concept of private advocacy, and then to find one or more of them who are so well convinced of the merits of the advocacy concept that they are willing to pay YOU to fulfill it for them.

Of course, one of the biggest hurdles we run into as private advocates is that most people have no idea our profession exists. They don't realize that when they encounter problems with their medical care or bills that such help might be available to them.

If they don't know we exist then how will they ever know to go looking for us, or to call us and hire us?

Consider this scenario...

> You've decided to establish a new rose garden in your backyard. You draw up your plans, figure out where it needs to be located, and grab your shovel to get started. As you ram the shovel into the dirt, you hit something that feels like a large rock. You move your shovel over a few inches to try again, realizing you'll need to shovel around that rock in order to remove it from your new garden. Ramming the shovel into the dirt once again, you feel the clunk! of a second rock... so you move over and try again. After a few minutes you realize the rock must be huge because you

keep running into it. Undaunted you begin digging around the perimeter of where you think that rock must be until – wait – one of them just shifted... You keep going until finally you can reach down into the dirt and... WHOA! What's this? It's perfectly round, heavy, rusty... if you didn't know any better you would think it was an old... cannonball !?! And wait... there seem to be several of them...

What on earth?... Are you kidding? ... A cannonball? Well, OK, you know Civil War skirmishes took place near your home in Mapledale. And, your home was built on land formerly part of an old farm that had been used as a post for the militia...

But – what do you do now? You can't keep cannonballs in your backyard! Or – are you even sure they are cannonballs? If they are, can they still explode? Is there a risk to having them so close by? Who can you ask? Who can identify these rusty, heavy round things, and might know what you can do to get rid of them?

Or – do they have any value? After all, they would be antiques. And... OK... now what about you supposed to do about your new rose garden?

As you gather your wits about you and try to figure out are to do next, you remember that last month at one of your weekly Rotary meetings, there was a speaker who was a Civil War buff. He spoke on "Mapledale's Little Known Civil War Secrets," and shared his interest in the Civil War, the re-enactments he participates in, some of the history that relates to Mapledale, and the artifacts he has been collecting ever since he was a teenager.

Bingo! Now you know where to start. You'll call him and ask him to stop by to check out these round, heavy, rusty balls in your backyard. Even if he doesn't know all the answers, he's a great resource to start with.

I know – you're wondering what on earth rose gardens, cannonballs and Civil War buffs have to do with patient advocacy and public speaking, right? It's a metaphor of course. Here's your answer:

Every day, people's lives are interrupted by something totally unexpected – like a bad fall, or strange symptoms which result in a scary diagnosis, a medical bill for thousands of dollars, or a call from an elderly parent who needs help immediately. Those interruptions, of course, are not unlike cannonballs. They require immediate attention, skills or knowledge those people don't have, and a realization they need help.

How will they know where to turn?

Getting the Word Out – Fast!

Only a small percentage of the general public knows what to do if they find a cannonball in their backyard. (Do you?) It's possible an even smaller percentage knows what to do if they find themselves caught in the unforgiving vice grip of the healthcare system, desperate for help with no knowledge of where to turn.

So, how can they learn that such help is available when they need it? How do they learn where to turn when their rose gardens are interrupted by health scares or challenges which throw them into the realization that they need help?

It's up to us, as the professionals we are, to teach them. It's our job to create that awareness.

So how do we do that? There are two ways to do so. We can connect with one person at a time. Or we can teach more than one person at a time, by speaking to larger groups.

Which way do you think can get the word out quicker? Which one will help grow your practice quicker? Which one will mean the message about what private advocacy can do to take care of those health-related cannonballs will expand even faster and further?

You know the answer. This can't surprise you. It's simple math.

You can reach out to one person at a time. Then that person will talk to another so then two people will know what kind of work you do and how you can help them. In a month's time you might reach 10 people who reach another 10 – so now 20 people will better understand advocacy, your work and how it can help them.

Or you can speak to a handful of groups in that same month. Maybe 10 people in one group, only 5 in another, but 30 in a third group. That means in the same month you've spoken to 45 people –more than twice as many. They will also mention your work to their friends... that's potentially 90 people who will now know what you do – in only one month.

Let's do some more math. Let's say (an educated guess) that in order to engage ONE client, you will need to speak to, say, 50 people who are part of your target audience, and who will also speak to their friends.

In scenario one, where you speak to only 10 of those folks, it will take you 5 months to gain a client. And that's assuming you do everything right when you talk to that person, set up your pricing and your contract, provide the necessary customer service ahead of the sale, and more.

In scenario two, where you speak to 45 people in a month, by our assumed average, it will take you just over one month to gain that same client. Even if you have trouble getting them to sign a contract, if you keep up your public speaking calendar, then it shouldn't even take you two full months.

Weigh that: 5 months – vs – 1+ months.

Do you have 5 months to wait for a new client to sign a contract with you?

Now consider whether it's worthwhile to attempt the public speaking plunge even if you're a bit fearful on the front end.

More About That Math

One of the big problems with public speaking isn't about the talk or the audience. It's about us, ourselves. We don't do a good job of managing our own expectations.

(By the way; this is true no matter what kind of marketing we are talking about. It just seems to be multiplied when it comes to public speaking.)

See if this rings a bell:

You prepare to give a talk; you create slides, practice the narrative, create a good handout to leave behind, show up on time and give a talk. You have an attentive audience, they ask good questions, they chat with you afterwards, they take your handouts, and you walk away knowing you've done a great job of teaching them about the topic at hand.

Then you return to your office... but the phone doesn't ring. No email requests arrive. And you think you have failed.

No wonder you don't want to do public speaking!

But you would be wrong about failure. You haven't failed in the talk you have given at all. The only thing you have failed to do is to recognize that it will take some time, and some additional outreach, to make sure those people who listened to your talk actually will get in touch with you when they need to. They aren't ready today! They don't have a challenge that requires your help today! But they might have that challenge tomorrow, or next week, or next year.

Let's go back to the cannonballs to see why it works this way. When you heard that Civil War buff speak, it was interesting enough, but it never occurred to you that you would ever need to connect with a Civil War buff. You learned something, your brain processed the information, but you didn't need a cannonball retriever or Civil War expert, so why would you care about remembering any more than just the basics?

Similarly, when you speak to others about the healthcare system and your advocacy work, no matter how large or small the group, few if any of the people in your audiences will expect to need your services, nor do they think they will be calling you right away. The last things they may be expecting are medical problems – OR cannonballs. Yes, it's possible they know of a reason to connect with you immediately, and the reality is that the more group talks you give, the more apt you are to find that person who will hire you before 24 hours go by.

But you can't expect that to happen. Or, please know that if you do expect it, you will most likely be sorely disappointed.

So if they aren't going to contact you right away, what can you do to maximize the chance they will contact you in the future?

We'll take a look at those tactics beginning on page 83.

A Word about "Groups"

Before we go further into the "how to's" let's make sure we define "groups."

Most people who really dislike the prospect of public speaking picture "giving a speech" as if it needs to be performed from the stage of an intimidatingly large auditorium full of hundreds (make that thousands!) of people who will be hanging on every word from their mouths, will be ready to test them through impossible-to-ask questions afterward, and will judge every movement, every word, every mannerism they observe throughout the process.

I promise you right here that if you ever get to the point where you have so many people in such a large space, then it will signal that you've made it into a speaking arena that you will have earned due to your expertise. Those are scenarios that invoke paid speaking gigs, usually from experts who have come in from out of town for a specific sort of event like a conference or convention. Rarely do those kinds of opportunities come along for someone who is giving talks about their profession on the level most advocates will ever provide.

Instead, the groups you will want to speak to, and will find opportunities for, are far more manageable and far, far less daunting. It's not about getting in over your head. It's simply a matter of a tiny step out of your comfort zone. You aren't leaping chasms to do this. You're crossing cracks in the sidewalk.

A "group" can be as small as a group of friends who get together for coffee – maybe 3 to 5 people in a living room. Or it might be as large as a few dozen people in a bigger room, like a fellowship hall in a church or a meeting hall at the Elks Club. It might be a group comprised of only people you have invited yourself, (like a Tupperware Party for advocacy) or it might be made up of an organization of people you have never met, and they have invited you, or accepted your proposal, to speak to their membership.

You may sit alongside attendees in a chair or on a couch, or even at a kitchen table. Or you may stand in front of the room – or at the back of the room while they look at slides on a screen.

All of these would be considered "public speaking" or "speaking opportunities." You can get started anywhere in that spectrum you would like to, depending on your comfort level. They are all groups, as we define groups for public speaking purposes.

Don't put yourself in a position to do much more than you feel comfortable doing initially. On the other hand, if you feel you have mastered one level of group speaking, then test the next level. Aspire to larger groups as you go along.

Remember your math! The more people you speak to, the more likely you will find the one who needs you – if not immediately, then soon.

A Word About Frequency

Finally, dare I say to you – don't overdo it! If you end up with too many speaking opportunities, and end up with too much business all at once, that's not good either.

Balance in all things.

Early in your practice, you'll want to do as much speaking to groups as possible to begin building your practice to a level that keeps you just busy "enough" – based on your own definition of enough. As you get busier, don't stop speaking! Anticipate that the number of hours you devote to your clients will slow down as you complete projects, and do some more speaking six or eight weeks prior to that. Once you ramp up to a good balance between the time your clients need and the time you've got, be sure to leave room in your schedule to continue your marketing. Included will be additional speaking opportunities. In fact, if done right, along with regular word-of-mouth from your clients, your own website, and your AdvoConnection Directory listing (www.AdvoConnection.com) , you may not need to do any other form of marketing.

• How many suggested speaking opportunities?

A. If you are just getting started in practice and trying to build clientele:

Schedule talks to cover 50+ people to find one client who will hire you within the next two months.[13] (That means one talk to 50+ people, or two talks to 25+ people each, or four talks to 12+ people each, etc.) If you want to be working for two clients, then you'll need to schedule talks to cover 100 people. Three clients will require 150+ people and so forth.

B. Once you find yourself with a good balance of clients against the time you have to help them (your billable hours), and If you are still within your first 2 or 3 years of practice and find your clientele level to be up and down (too many clients this month, not enough work next month), or you are working for too many clients who don't fit the niche you are trying to build:

Then schedule talks to cover 100+ people per month on a steady basis, and begin choosing the ones you will work with to fit your niche the best. The key is that the more people you expose your work to through speaking, the more likely you are to find mostly clients who fit your niche, as long as your topic also fits your niche.

C. If you have been in practice for a while, and are hoping to simply keep a steady stream of clients:

---

13 Fifty people to find one client is an educated guestimate. Your mileage may vary depending on your niche and your track record. You won't know whether the first person you speak to will hire you, or number 50, or which one in between. This would be an average.

Then try to keep doing at least one talk per month, but be sure to focus it directly on the niche you are building, if any.

D. If you are hoping to add additional advocacy personnel to your company, then you'll want to go back to the beginning – see A – as if you are just getting started, although you'll morph into the B approach pretty quickly.

If you are one of those folks who truly does not like to do public speaking, I beg you to just give it a try on a scale that makes you comfortable. Each time you are successful, it will make you a bit more confident; a bit bolder. Soon you'll have the confidence and skills of a champion, and your practice will be busy.

Public Speaking Planning – Making It Happen and Getting It Done

Hopefully I've made the case that public speaking is a great way to build your client list and to fill your available billable hours.

Now it's time to get down to the nitty gritty – the "how to." Here we'll look at how to:

A. Determine what to talk about

B. Find speaking opportunities and schedule them

C. Prepare for the talk you give

D. Create a handout to leave behind

E. Capture names and contact information

F. Follow up: short-term and longer-term

A. What Are You Supposed to Talk About?

Once you've been on the speaking circuit for a while, you may find that groups approach you asking you to speak on a specific topic.

But until then you'll need to come up with your own ideas for titles and topics so you can propose them to meeting planners. The choices you make should be aimed at accomplishing a handful of things:

1. Sparking enough interest for the person who will "book" your talk (usually an organization's meeting chairperson) to be willing to put you on the schedule.

2. Sparking enough interest among possible attendees so that they will show up to hear you speak.

3. The topic should be narrow enough that people will have an idea of what they are going to learn. (You wouldn't use "healthcare" as a topic – way too broad. You also wouldn't use "getting help for people with brain tumors" – because that is way too narrow.)

4. The topic should be broad enough so that they will have learned something they never knew before – including how a patient or health advocate (like you!) can help them.

5. Your only real goal in speaking is to entice someone to pick up the phone to call you, or send you an email – but of course it will require 1-4 above to make that happen. Your overall posture is that you want listeners to TRUST you when you have finished speaking. You want them to believe that YOU are the EXPERT who can help them get what they need. YOU and no one else can relieve their FUDGE.[13]

So, with those parameters, how can you craft a great title and topic?

This may surprise you, but you won't be talking about patient advocacy. Well, at least that won't be the main topic or the title of your talk. Your work and abilities as an advocate will get woven into the story you tell; they just won't be the focus of it.

Instead, the title and subject of your talk need to be something that sparks the interest of the person who will listen. When someone hears your title, you want them to think, "Oh yes, that sounds like something I would like to hear." Or – at least they won't dismiss it, or think it sounds boring. As much as you and I hold patient advocacy near and dear to our hearts, not everyone else does (I know – hard to believe!) It's up to us to choose a few topics, and craft interesting-enough titles that we know the members of our target audiences will jump at the chance to listen to us speak. (Or at least they won't run away.)

Here's an example: do you remember the title our Civil War speaker chose, "Mapledale's Little Known Civil War Secrets"? Even if you didn't think you had much interest in the Civil War, you would at least show up to listen to his talk, because everyone loves to hear a secret! That's your goal for your topic, too; to find something that will spark interest.

Here are some advocacy related examples. See if they fit our parameters:

Target Audience	Ideas: Titles and Topics
Patients and caregivers	*Keeping Yourself Safe in the Hospital* This title suggests that not everyone IS safe (they aren't) and that there are some ways patients or caregivers can improve safety (there are.)

---

13 FUDGE = Fear, uncertainty, doubt, guilt, and exhaustion. More about FUDGE can be found in Chapter Five – Expanding Your Target Audiences.

Target Audience	Suggested Titles and Topics
Cont.	*Cont.*
Patients and caregivers	*Secrets to Finding Credible Health Information Online* This title suggests that not all health information found online is credible (it's not) and that there are some ways to find useful information (there are.)
Patients and caregivers	*Uncovering Mistakes in Your Medical Bills* This title suggests that – what? – there are mistakes in medical bills? (Yes, I'm being facetious.) You can expose some of those dirty little medical billing "mistakes" – certainly an enticing title. But of course, be sure you mention at the end that those are just a few of the "errors" you look for – there are many more.
Employers	*Saving Money and Keeping Your Employees on the Job: A New Approach to Medical Care* Discuss absenteeism, presenteeism, reviewing hospital and other medical bills, and anything else that speaks to an employer saving money and grief. This talk would most likely be given by a medical billing and claims advocate.
Financial Planners	*Growing Client Investments Through Healthcare Support* Speaking to financial planners as a secondary audience can lead you toward helping their clients. (Remember, as reviewed in Chapter Five, financial advisors are always looking for ways to help their clients invest more money.)

You are welcome to use these titles, or create your own, of course. In particular, if you are developing a niche, you'll want to develop a talk that will help you shine as the expert in your area of expertise.

Once you've found a title and topic you like, you'll need to create a marketing description for your talk. Just a few sentences that the meeting planner can use on the group's website, or in a newsletter. It's like an elevator pitch[14] for your speech. Remember to focus on the benefits to the listener of what you will say. It should both reveal the gist of what you'll talk about, and leave some question marks, too, so listeners will be eager to hear the answers.

Here is an example of a description a meeting planner would want you to supply for a talk called *Secrets to Finding Credible Health Information Online.*

---

14 Find a thorough discussion of elevator pitches in *The Health Advocate's Basic Marketing Handbook.*

Snake oil salesmen are alive and well and thriving online. Are you or a loved one falling for their misinformation? Or do you know instead how verify information you find, making sure it's credible and useful?

Suzie Speaker, professional patient advocate and owner of Starlight Health Advocacy, will teach us to recognize when the truth has been twisted to entice us to buy that snake oil. Then she'll give us a handful of tools to help us verify truly useful information.

Exercise – Developing Your Talk Idea

Using the guidelines I've just laid out for you, develop a topic, title and description for a talk you might propose to give.

Begin by picturing a small group of ten or twelve people sitting around a table with you at the head. What would they want to learn from you? What would you want to teach them? What topic would help them walk away knowing they have learned something new, that they now trust you because you taught it to them, and that calling you to support them with advocacy services would be a smart choice?

Excellent. Now you have a great topic and title in mind, and your description is ready... let's delve into the nitty gritty of rounding up speaking opportunities.

B. Finding and Scheduling Speaking Opportunities

Unless you plan to do all your talks in your own living room, you will need to identify, contact, and coordinate with a meeting planner or program chairperson for the groups you will speak to. These are the people you will need to convince that you're a great choice for a meeting speaker, then arrange the details to make it all happen.

Where do you find these people? It's not nearly as difficult as you might think.

Start by making a list of organizations in your area that look for guest speakers, like community and civic groups. Most like to have speakers at their meetings, and they like to present a variety of topics. Some even have attendance requirements, which means you'll have a guaranteed attendance.

I once heard Garth Brooks call these organizations the "animal circuit;" – you know – the Elks, the Moose, the Lions. I'm not sure how "animal" they are, but you can add the Rotary, Kiwanis, Optimists, the Chamber of Commerce, business networking groups and others. Churches and synagogues often have interest groups you could speak to, too.

If you have a specific niche you'd like to talk about, you might find out if there are support groups that would have that specific interest and would invite you as a guest. Connect with your local hospital or other organizations that sponsor or support these groups.

You can find a master list of potential speaking opportunities and organizations in the Online Resource Bank (ORB). **ORB**

Find the contact information you need by searching online for your city or town, and the name of the group. There will be a phone number or email address you can reach out to. Ask your network of friends and family if they are members, or know someone who can help you get a foot in the door to any of these groups.

My only warning is: don't get carried away making too many contacts at first. Once you begin speaking and people appreciate what you have to say, you'll be in demand without having to make many connections yourself at all. Not only do people who belong to one organization (and hear you speak) belong to other organizations (and share your information with those planners) but meeting planners also seem to have their own little underground to help them ferret out speakers, too. Your phone will begin to ring without much more effort on your part.

I would go so far as to say that once you have spoken to four or five groups, you may never need to make another phone call to a meeting planner.

As you get started, you may need to contact more than one person per organization, as you hone in on the meeting planner / decision maker him or herself. Sometimes the contact information online is old, or is just a general email address. You may call one person only to find out he was last year's planner, so he'll supply you with this year's planner's information.... Eventually you'll find THE person who schedules guest speakers. Your persistence will pay off.

So what do you say to them? Use a script like this, or edit it for email, tailored to your own information, of course.

> *Hi _____. My name is Suzie Speaker. I'm a private health advocate here in the _____ area, and am seeking opportunities to help others learn about the benefits of working with professionals to help them navigate the healthcare system. I've put together a program called _____ (your title) _____ to help members of the _____ (organization name)_____ better understand how to _____.*
>
> *If you are looking for speakers in the next several months, I can make myself available. Is that something you are interested in?"*

It may be that simple. The planner will pull out his calendar – and off you go. Or, they may ask you to submit a written request, or a link to your website. Or it could be they report to a meeting committee. Eventually they will get back to you.

A good meeting organizer seeks a variety of topics for his or her organization and will want to discuss the subject matter with you. That's why we went through the title and topic exercise earlier. Now you'll know just how to discuss it.

Don't be surprised if you are scheduled six or more months in advance; that's how most meeting planners work. If you hope to speak sooner than that, then offer to pinch hit if one of their already scheduled speakers needs to cancel.

Once you know you've got the gig, be sure to ask for details, like the time and place, what the dress is, whether they prefer you bring a PowerPoint or not (and if so, if they have a projector you can use), approximately how many people will attend (so you can bring the right number of hand-outs), and very important – how long they would want you to speak.

C. Prepare the Talk You Will Give

So – it's a date! And now it's time to prepare the talk you will give.

Because every talk and audience are so different, I won't attempt here to show you how to prepare the actual content of what you will say.

But I can give you some guidelines for crafting your speech to ensure your audiences feel well-served, and to be sure the results are just what you've planned for: to make your phone ring and your email sing.

Start by thinking about the best talks and speeches you've ever heard. What did you like about them? Would you want to hear that speaker again? Why?

The answers to those questions will lie within the following best practices:

• Content and Questions

Know your subject. Read everything you can get your hands on about it. Know the pros and cons of the main arguments so you can help your audience understand different points of view. Remember small details that will strike others as being interesting. Confidence in your knowledge of your subject matter will go a long way toward your audience's trust in you when you are finished.

Don't worry about supplying every detail known to man on your subject. An overview is all you need. Minutia will bog you down unless it causes amazement, or provides a quotable quote, or a detail your listener will want to tell someone else later. Instead, leaving a few holes in your talk invites questions – interactivity! – and that's a much preferred outcome.

No matter how well you know your subject matter, there will be times you don't know the answer to a question. When someone stumps you, tell them what a great question they have asked, that you don't know the answer, but if they will leave their email address with you, you will try to find the answer will reply to them with it.

At the same time you feel confident in your subject matter, be willing to listen to new ideas. Audience members will ask questions about something they have read or heard. If you are familiar and can elaborate – great! But they also love it when you, the confident expert, admits, "You know, I've never heard that before! Thank you for sharing it with me! I'm going to look for more information." It makes them feel respected and useful. Further, you aren't endorsing it or naysaying it – you're just providing feedback.

Most importantly, even though your topic won't be about advocacy per se, be sure to weave not just the story of private advocacy into your talk, but your specific expertise into it, too. After all, that's your reason for doing this talk to begin with! When you are finished, you want people to say that they heard a *patient advocate* speak on the topic of X.

• Delivery

Nobody wants to listen to a robot. Your delivery should be enthusiastic, friendly and informal, more like a conversation than a speech. Make eye contact with people in the audience. Smile. Refer to notes if necessary, but don't read them. Be at least mildly animated (although don't do a lot of talking with your hands – that can get annoying.) Ask questions and nod or shake your head to indicate you expect a wholesale audience response. Ask for a show

Can You Get Paid for Speaking?

The short answer is yes.

But whether or not you should expect to be paid for giving a presentation depends on several factors:

1. If you are doing the outreach to meeting planners requesting an invitation, then your compensation will be their "yes," your ability to address a captive group of potential clients, and the name and contact information gold you leave with. Don't expect them to pay you.

2. If instead you are asked to speak to a civic, business or any other local group, consider the group making the request. If it is a local community, church/synagogue, or business networking group then they probably have no budget for speakers. They'll be happy to let you collect contact information like in #1, and that will be your compensation. The exposure to those audiences may be worth the effort.

3. If a group asks you to participate as an expert, and they will be making money from people who have paid admission to attend the conference or meeting, then by all means, ask to be paid. If it requires out-of-town travel, then ask to be compensated for all travel expenses too. Sign a contract with them to be sure you'll be paid what you negotiate.

4. Sometimes you may be asked to speak as an expert, but they won't pay an honorarium or speaker fee, instead offering you "free admission" to their conference or program. In these cases they may, or may not pick up your travel expenses. When that kind of offer comes along you'll need to decide on your own whether what you get from the opportunity (exposure, new clients, making connections, information gathering) are worth the cost to you in time and money.

My rules of thumb might work for you too. I never charge local groups unless they are like #3 above. If I am asked to speak out of town, I always ask for travel expense coverage, and usually ask to be paid to speak too. My speaker fees range from $500 to $3500 depending on the topic and the group, and the purpose the group has for the meeting or conference. If they are a for-profit meeting company, I ask top dollar. If they turn me down, then it wasn't worth my time anyway.

of hands on occasion. The more interactive you make your talk, the more apt you are to keep your audience's attention.

Don't stand behind a podium! That puts an unfriendly boundary between you and your audience. Walk around in the front of the room, or, if you are using slides, stand in the back of the room and let them look at the slides projected on the front wall.

Speak loudly enough for everyone to hear, but don't yell. If yelling is the only way they can hear you, then you really need to use a microphone. If so, ask for a handheld mike, or a lavalier mike (one that hangs around your neck, or pins to your blouse, shirt or lapel).

Q & A will be an important part of your talk, but you'll want to determine ahead of time whether you will accept questions during the talk, or whether you prefer people wait until you have finished your presentation. Sometimes your meeting planner will tell you their group's preference on this. One way isn't better than the other, but it can affect the amount of time it takes for you to deliver the entire presentation.

Time is your friend and your enemy! You'll never finish exactly on time, so err by coming up just a few minutes short, inviting time for more questions. Running long is almost always a problem. Practice your talk so that you use up about 80% of your allotted speaking time. I guarantee you it will take you longer to deliver than you think it will.

If you plan to use PowerPoint slides or any other display, decide whether you will use your own equipment, or if the meeting planner will provide equipment you can use. I prefer to use my own laptop (because sometimes I use funky fonts in my PowerPoint that don't render correctly on someone else's computer). You may need only to copy your PowerPoint to a thumb drive, so you can use their equipment.

Remember, too, that if you use a laptop presentation, you'll also need a projector. Many groups have one you can use, but be sure to ask. If you know you will be doing a lot of speaking with your laptop, you may want to purchase your own projector (cost = $350+).

If you haven't spent much time creating slides, then be sure to read up on best practices for doing so. The emphasis should be on guiding and enhancing a talk, but not including all the words you will use as you give it. (I've shared one of my patient-focused talks in the ORB so you can see how the content and images are done to just enhance the talk, not cover it completely.) **ORB**

And whatever you do – don't read the slides!

However you decide to use equipment, the key is to practice your delivery with the equipment you'll be using ahead of time. Murphy's Law rears its ugly head when you don't.

D. Create a handout to leave behind

So you've delivered your talk. Everyone applauded. Now they are getting up to go home. The meeting planner has thanked you for doing a good job. You're picking up your equipment or putting materials back into your briefcase. Now what?

Do NOT, under any circumstances, let your audience members leave without taking materials you've created for them with them. A flyer, some SWAG (Stuff We All Get – like branded pens or tablets), even a coupon for your services. (Get one hour of service free with the purchase of four hours!) Be sure whatever you give them has your name, your company's name, your logo, your web address, email address and phone number easily found.

I've provided a sample handout in the ORB – one that goes with the sample presentation mentioned in the last sub-section of this chapter. (ORB)

Providing them with take-home materials may be the second most important part of your talk.

Even more important than not letting them leave without your materials, is not letting them leave until you...

E. Capture their names and contact information

Why did you go to all this trouble to speak to this group? You've just shared your time and expertise with them, so you have a right to ask them for something in return. Which takes us to the most important part of your talk – capturing their names and contact information.

Almost every person who attends a talk you give is either a potential client or an influencer, so acquiring their names and contact information is like panning for gold.

There are many ways to ask for that information. You can simply pass around a clip board with a pen attached—maybe they will sign it, or maybe not. Or you can do a drawing for a free gift, asking them to fill out the drawing slip with their name and email address. Collect all those slips, draw the winner's name, and keep all the slips to add to your outreach lists after you return to your office.

The "free gifts" don't have to be anything expensive. I give away a copy of my book[15] which was written for patients. You might find a book you think a winner would like, or even a $10 gift card to Amazon or Starbucks – whatever you think. People are thrilled to win anything and once again, it garners trust.

Remember our discussion of building your platform in Chapter Four? Meeting all these folks, and making them a part of your four legged-stool is definitely a platform builder.

---

15 You Bet Your Life! The 10 Mistakes Every Patient Makes (How to Fix Them to Get the Healthcare You Deserve)

F. Follow up: short-term and longer-term

Your talk is over. It was a success. But there's no time to rest on your laurels.

Within the next 24 hours, you have two tasks.

- First, you're going to connect with those attendees by email right away, striking while the iron is hot, thanking them for being such a great audience, providing links to follow up information, and making sure they know you are ready and able to serve their advocacy needs.

   Even better than a simple thank you is development of a survey, asking for feedback on your performance. You can create one using a free survey tool online (ORB) that asks whether they learned anything new, what they did or didn't like about your delivery. Keep it simple and short, let them answer it anonymously, but overall you might learn something about your speech-giving skills that will help you be even better then next time.

- And second, you're going to add all those names and email addresses to your master list of potential clients. There will be many things you can use these contacts for, like development of your newsletter, or invitations to join you in social media. Many of these tactics are discussed later in this book.

-

Measuring Your Success

So how do we measure public speaking? There are a few ways we know we're headed in the right direction:

1. Collection of email addresses: If you have collected names and email addresses from 75% or more of your attendees, then consider your talk a success.

2. Phone calls or follow up from attendees: Even if they don't plan to hire you right away, the fact that they engaged post-talk is very positive; it shows that you garnered their trust. They may only have interest in a conversation or clarification at first, but they clearly value your expertise or they would not have followed up.

3. A call from another organization: as described earlier, groups love to know about new speakers, and there seems to be a "circuit" in any given town. If someone mentions another group they belong to after you've delivered your talk, or if you get a follow up phone call or email, then that is another mark of success.

4. Website or blog pageviews: We'll look more closely at websites in the next chapter, but one way of measuring success is to see if your pageviews go up within the 48 hours after a talk, or right after you send a follow up email. If there is further interest in what you had to say, you'll see a marked increase.

So that's it – the overview to being a great public speaker in the advocacy arena, using public speaking as the way to propel the growth of your business.

Don't forget to check out the Online Resource Bank (ORB) **ORB** for additional resources that will help you grow your speaking capabilities and successes.

Chapter Eight

Tactic: Refining Your Website

This tactic will:

- Support every marketing strategy you develop
- Provide a clear all to action to all audiences
- Extend your branding
- Raise your website authority in search engines

Considering "the web" to be one marketing medium is like saying paper is one medium. In fact, paper is used to develop many tools: flyers, business cards, newspapers, magazines posters even most billboards – they are all made from paper.

And so it is true with the Internet, or the web (for our purposes, they are the same thing.) The web can be used for many forms of marketing including websites, web advertising, PR, blogging, social media and others. There is no question that tactical use of the web will help your target audiences find you. It is imperative that you maximize your use of them all, channeling your efforts and most of your marketing budget toward them.

In these next few chapters we are going to look at five of those uses:

- This chapter, Chapter Eight, will cover some advanced website information (to supplement the more extensive information found in *The Health Advocate's Basic Marketing Handbook*.)

- Chapter Nine will review blogging. It's important enough that it needs its own chapter.

- Chapter Ten will address social media. Of course, social media changes so quickly that it may be out of date before you get your hands on this book! (But then, that's one reason I've built the ORB **ORB** – to keep you updated.)

- Then, in Chapter Eleven we are going to look at email newsletters.

- Finally, in Chapter Twelve we'll look at a few miscellaneous tactics including web advertising, online support groups, article writing and more.

So let's get started by looking at your own website.

The basics of website development were covered quite well in *The Health Advocate's Basic Marketing Handbook*. There we looked at the types of information that are must-haves, and how to be sure the search engines can find and categorize your website (SEO = Search Engine Optimization.)

The overall goal, of course, is to be visible and professional in your web presentation, making it very easy for a prospective client to learn just enough to pick up the phone and make contact. Meta-descriptions and authority help them find you.

So now let's take a look at some advanced theory on websites. Beyond the basics, what do you need to know to be sure potential clients find you online and pick up the phone?

Computers Now Have Legs

The first, and most important -- and newest – change is that people aren't just using desktop or even laptop computers to access the web. Increasingly they are accessing the web with phones and tablets, and on the near horizon – digital watches. These mobile devices are found everywhere, come in every size, and all have different view requirements for your web content.

This creates all new programming challenges because it's no longer just about creating a website. Now it's about creating several versions of the same information, possibly formatting them differently for each type of device. What looks good on a computer with a 1920 wide pixel monitor won't look the same on a tablet or phone with monitors that are 360x480. And most text and images that are readable on a computer monitor will be too tiny on a tablet or smartphone. (I can't even imagine how small it looks on one of those little watches!)

And, don't think it's only youngsters who are using all these devices. Once my own doctor's practice implemented electronic health records, she gleefully reported to me that her older patients (75+) were using their iPads to connect with her!

So sizing and readability becomes more important than ever before. For example, the size of text and its readability are very important if your advocacy work is targeted to older folks with vision challenges or anyone who is visually impaired. Also, very large images are bandwidth hoggers. If someone tries to access your information with slow internet access (found in rural areas or from dial-up or satellite internet providers) then they may grow impatient waiting for your information to show up on their monitors no matter what size they are – and move on.

Therefore, accommodations need to be made for all these different presentations of our content. Whereas in the "old" days we tried to include as much information as possible on a homepage so people wouldn't have to click too many times to find what they needed, now the movement is toward simplicity, with fewer elements on every page, but with the basics still front and center, recognizing that most of the people who are looking for us just want to figure out quickly whether:

1. we can help them (benefits and services)
2. we are located within the right geography to be helpful to them
3. they can afford to work with us

With those questions satisfied, they may simply want to click on your phone number and dial from their device.

Fortunately, specialized programming can handle those variations, and the gurus who build websites know how to use it. If you don't have a website yet, or are planning on an overhaul of yours, then find one of these folks and ask them how they accommodate for the many-sized digital devices that customers and clients use these days.

For those of us who already have websites, and don't wish to pay to have them entirely rebuilt, there are some steps we can take to figure out whether or not we need to make any changes.

First, take a look at your website on as many devices as you can. Ask friends, family members and co-workers if you can borrow their devices, then look over your website; if possible, all pages of your website.

Ask yourself:

- Is it easy to read? (Is the text clear, and large enough for your target audiences?)
- When you try to click to another page, is the button or text large enough that it's not difficult to do?
- Are your phone number and email address front and center and easy to find without much scrolling around the page?

As long as you make sure mobile devices address those questions, then don't worry so much about the rest of your site. It's perfectly acceptable to have a homepage that adjusts to mobile devices while leaving the rest of your site the way it has been if it is already serving you well. A "deep dive" on your content is important for search engines, and will be found by someone who wants to know much more.

If you still aren't sure how important it might be to make adjustments for mobile devices, ask your webmaster to review your site analytics (see page 92). Among the data points you can get are what devices are being used, how fast their access is, even what operating systems they are using and who their services providers are. Most of that information won't be particularly useful to you, but it's always an interesting review.

The Biggest Changes in SEO

SEO = Search Engine Optimization was well-explained in *The Health Advocate's Basic Marketing Handbook* (Chapter Ten). Metadata, authority and other fine points of programming help Google, Bing, Yahoo and other search engines find you online and move you to the top of their SERPs (Search Engine Results Pages.)

The key words there are "find you online." Traditionally (which, given that search engines have only been around for 14 or 15 years, seems a bit of a stretch) if you wanted to search for something, you would choose your favorite search engine, type in a few keywords and voila! You would find a list of 1,253,677 links to something that approached the answer you were looking for.

But the advent of mobile devices has caused a huge shift in how those searches are done today. Today a search is just as apt to be done by voice (Ask Siri!) as it is by typing words, and that means the search may be done with phrases and sentences, not just keywords.

> Instead of typing: patient advocate Timbuktu

> Voice search will "hear"   "I need a patient advocate in Timbuktu."

Here's the good news: if you live and work in Timbuktu, and there aren't more than two or three other advocates working in your area, then those search engines are going to produce a link to your website near the top of the SERPs (Search Engine Results Pages) no matter whether the search was done by typing or speaking.

But if the search is for a patient advocate in Boston, or one in Los Angeles, the Bay Area or Miami, or another area where there are already a dozen or more practicing advocates, then preparing your metatags for voice search might make a difference on where you appear on the SERP. If somewhere in your text or your metatags, you actually write the sentence, "I need a patient advocate in Boston" then you have a better chance of ending up at the top.

The only "next step" beyond voice I can think of is when our tablets and smartphones begin reading our minds, so we only have to think of the question or statement and the results will be delivered to us. But for now, let's not worry about that one. (It gives me the creeps anyway.)

Here a Web, There a Web, Everywhere a Web, Web

Having just one presence on the web is oh, so 1998. Today it makes more sense to be accessible in many places online, probably more places than you might realize.

For example, beyond your practice's website (1), you may also have a listing page in the AdvoConnection Directory (2), a Linked In profile (3), a Facebook page (4), a blog (5) and other social media and profile listings. (6, 7, 8 and more?)

But have you considered building a second website all together? Or even a third? (11 and 12?)

Creating more than one website makes great sense in a couple of cases:

- If you decide to establish yourself as an expert (Chapter Four), then you will want to have your business website, plus an entirely different website to showcase your expertise. They will link to each other, of course, and you might even share some of their pages, but they have two distinctly different goals and therefore should have different, although related, online presences. I have my Every Patient's Advocate website and I have a Trisha Torrey website. Even though much of the content is similar, and they share some branding, they have different purposes.

- If your work addresses distinctly different audiences and the benefits messages aren't the same, you may want to create one website for each audience. A good example of this is a legal nurse consultant who is also a patient advocate. Her legal nurse consulting business speaks to an entirely different audience with entirely different interests from the patients who might hire her; thus she has two different websites. They do link to each other. But they are very different in look, content and metadata.

If you decide you need more than one website, consider:

- There are new domain extensions available you can make use of when choosing your name. (Domain extensions are .com, .net, .org, .us, .ca and so forth.) Dozens of new domains were approved by ICANN, the domain police for use beginning in 2014. They may be a great boon to the website builders of this world, or they may cause great confusion. It will be a few years before we know the real effect. But that doesn't mean you shouldn't use them. For example, you might want to be JaneAdvocate.guru or PatientAdvocate.associates or Patient.help -- yes, .guru, .associates, and .help are all new domain (ORB) extensions that can be registered and used. Check the ORB for more information.

- Be sure all your sites and other web presences link to all the others. That's just smart marketing and good practice. Even if all you do is link to them from a Resources page, they can support each other with extra "google juice"[16], helping you rank a bit higher in the SERPs.

General Website Advice

- When building your new site(s) keep in mind the previous advice about using phraseology instead of just keywords. That might mean you do some FAQs or Q&A on your site.

- Include your own photo, and the photos of anyone else in your company who will call on clients, on your "About Us" page. This builds trust – so much more so than a photo of a model who has no relationship to your practice.

- Branding: think carefully about whether you want all your web presences to have the same look and feel. If your brand messages and promises have similarities (good quality, expertise, peace of mind, etc) then repeating your brand is a good approach.

---

16 Google juice is another term the extra authority or trust that might improve your page rank, important to help you move higher up in **SERPs** (Search Engine Results pages.)

- Content: when considering the information you will add to your site, don't try to tell everything you know. Your goal is to get someone to pick up the phone and call, or to send you an email. If you answer too many questions, then they may decide not to call – because you've answered all the questions. Instead, include just enough information so they know you can probably help them, but not so much information that they dismiss you before they dial or type.

- Since you've probably been in practice for a while (one of our assumptions from the Introduction to this book), you have hopefully collected some testimonials and endorsements from clients. Your website is a great place to showcase them!

Measuring Your Success

Of course, the most important measurement of your website's effectiveness is counting how many times the phone rings.

But beyond phone calls....

I have plenty of beefs with Google, but one of the very best things they have done for those of us with websites is to develop Google Analytics. If you want to measure the success of your website, Google Analytics is all you need.

You can learn how many people have visited your site (pageviews, formerly called "hits"), which pages they landed on from search engines, where they came from (called referrers), which page was the last one they looked at, and then you can learn which ones found you from a computer vs a mobile device.

Ask your webmaster to add Google Analytics to all your websites, and then ask for a tutorial in how to use them to learn more about your visitors. If you find problems with the marketing performance of your site, they can be fixed.

Draw conclusions using the statistics you find there. For example, if you find out that most people land on a page other than your homepage, then, try to figure out why, then consider moving that information to your homepage.

So that's it for Web Marketing and bringing your web presence up to date. None of it is rocket science. Most of it makes sense because it is marketing – not technology!.

Next up – blogging. It's an opportunity to really showcase your knowledge and expertise.

Chapter Nine

Tactic: Blogging

This tactic will:

- Extend both your personal brand (authority) and your business brand

- Raise your aura of expertise

- Raise your authority in search engines (if linked)

- Create trust among your audiences

Don't skip this chapter.

I know some of you will be tempted to skip it. You think blogging isn't something that applies to you. You don't consider yourself a good writer, or you don't like to deal with the technology. Or – the most wrong-minded excuse – that you don't have something important enough to say.

None of those excuses is good enough. And, particularly if you hope to become that expert we described in Chapter Four, know that you won't succeed without some way to showcase your expertise online. A blog is the shortest distance to that point.

A blog: is a collection of material (content) you share on the web that showcases and promotes your expertise and knowledge **on a continuing basis**. Your blog is the one central location where your updated, opinion-related, newsworthy content is housed.

A blog post: is one piece of the material you create and share. It might be written (text), image-based (infographics), audio (podcasts), or even video. In total all your posts together comprise your "**content**."

Blogging: is the activity of creating the content, usually considered to be text-based content, but could also be used for video (vlogs), audio or image posts.

The difference between a website and a blog is that word "continuing." A website lives online with static content that gets updated maybe every few months, or every few years, or never. A blog is updated on a regular, continual basis. (Some people update several times a day. Others once a week or even once a month.)

Why Is Blogging So Important?

If the business you were trying to grow, and the expertise you were hoping to establish, was about being the best pizza crafter and seller in your entire city, I would tell you that you probably don't need a blog.

But you are building an advocacy practice, and as we have read and discussed many times, advocacy is not a well-known profession yet. Few of us run practices that are so well known that we don't need to continually market them. Further, with constant changes in the healthcare landscape you have the unique opportunity to showcase your expertise on a variety of topics within healthcare, all of which contribute to what patients need to know.

There is much to share and teach our potential clients about the work we do. The nature of our work is that few potential clients think about it before they need it. They are often in crisis, in a state of FUDGE[16], and we need to be there, and available at the moment they decide they want the information. We can't be sitting in everyone's living room, in person, 24/7, to answer their questions when the need arises. So we need to do the next best thing – be at the other end of a mouse click.

Can it be done with just a website or a LinkedIn profile? Maybe. That's a good start.

But it your intent is to become a thought leader, an authority, recognized within your niche while promoting your work and expertise, influencing the way the profession and its regard will grow, then you need to blog. Further, unless you are willing to let your website slip in the SERPs (search engine results pages) then you must produce a continual flow of that expert content. Like potato chips, just one won't do.

Think of it another way:

Suppose you have an unusual legal question and you know you need to talk to a lawyer. You go online and find two lawyers who work nearby – one who has a website with some information about his practice on it, and the other who not only has that nice website, but also blogs about current thinking as it relates to your question...

Which of those lawyers do you regard as more of an expert? Which one would you be willing to pay more for?

---

16 FUDGE = fear, uncertainty, doubt, guilt and exhaustion. Read more in *The Health Advocate's Basic Marketing Handbook*.

Some Additional Reasons to Blog

One of the biggest differences between a website and a blog is like the difference between a brochure and a conversation.

A website or brochure includes statements of facts and/or promotional material intended to sell someone on hiring you for your services. It's a billboard or a poster. It's a one sided communication.

A blog or a conversation invites a two way, give and take, interactive relationship. It's a way for two people (or more) to connect and influence each other's thinking. It's not a billboard or a poster, it's a dialog, or maybe even a party. It can create a relationship.

Creating a relationship before someone even picks up the phone to talk to you about their needs and circumstances can help that potential client cross the bridge to hire you even before your phone conversation together begins. They've already begun to build trust.

Another reason to blog is because of the perspective it gives you. At first, you may find it difficult to think about the topics you'll write about. How many different ways can you say you'll sit by someone's bedside in the hospital?

But once you get started, maybe six or eight posts in, you'll notice that you begin to expand your thinking. You might begin to regard someone else's point of view differently, or you might better understand an experience you've had earlier in your own life, or maybe you'll begin to appreciate something you never thought about that way before... you'll do all of those because you'll ask yourself, "if I was going to blog about this, what would I say?"

All that extra thinking is incredibly healthy for your aura of expertness, your business – and even just your brain. You won't write about all those things. You may never even complete the thoughts. But I guarantee you that just like a painter begins to see the world around her in different colors and reflections, you will see your world from a new perspective as well.

As you might imagine, all these dimensions to blogging add up to the opportunity to learn more about your topic in ways you could not accomplish in any other way. Especially as you find more and more people commenting on your blog, or even just asking questions at the post, or in an email behind the scenes, you will learn a great deal that will expand your knowledge of your topic. That can only serve your clients well.

Finally, just from the sheer practice of regular writing, you will become a better writer. Yes, your spelling and punctuation will improve over time, but more than that, you'll find you formulate your ideas in a much more organized fashion, you explain your point of view much more clearly, and you get more comfortable with the process. Even if you don't consider yourself a good writer, don't let that stop you. You will get better!

How Much Time Does Blogging Require?

Forget all those "blogging is free" statements you see online. Yes, you can get a blog up and running and never write a check. But time is money, of course. There may be no out-of-pocket cost, but you'll spend plenty of time creating and maintaining a blog.

If someone wanted to pin down real numbers, I would say that a blog that will be truly useful to you will require 8 to 10 hours to get it set up, and to understand the basics of how it operates. Now, you can tinker with the colors, your branding, the layout and more and use up twice that! But count on at least those 8 to 10 to start.

Then you'll want to decide how frequently you will blog, and the time required will be affected by that. I've run four blogs at different times in the past ten years. One blog I only add to maybe once a month – no more than 2-3 hours a month. I used to post to another one 3-4 times a week! I spent easily 11-12 hours a week (44+ hours a month). I know some people who spend several hours a day, every day, blogging.

Your mileage will vary. As you get started, you'll take far more time. You'll feel this compulsion to make sure everything is perfect – perfect! Perfectionism takes time. Proofreading takes time. Correction and rewriting takes time.

But then, gradually, you'll become far more efficient. You'll start to edit yourself (making sure that what might have required 100 words last month can be said in only 65 this month.) When I go back to read my early blog posts (circa late 2005) I see how much I have evolved. But then, this is 2,000+ posts later.

You'll also get more comfortable. You'll find your "voice' – the "you" in your blog posts. Soon your blog will be a real reflection of YOU. YOU as the expert. YOU as the advocate. YOU as the business owner. YOU as someone who has something that is important enough that it's worth doing continually, and is appreciated by its readers – who become your eventual clients.

Getting Started – How to Set Up Your Blog

Hopefully I've convinced you that blogging is worth your while, both personally and for your practice. So let's get started.

(If you have already started a blog, and even if you've started one before and abandoned it, you may find some gems in here to help you.)

Step 1: Decide on your topic and your point of view.

Your topic is important because people want to know what they are going to read about. Like developing your niche, you need the Goldilocks approach – broad enough to give you plenty of room for writing, but not too broad because you'll get lost in the millions of blogs that already exist. You want a topic that is just right.

Your point of view is the way you look at your topic. An example would be choosing a topic of politics, and saying your point of view is red-state Republican.

Or another example from my experience. My TrishaTorrey.com blog is about patient empowerment. My point of view is that I help you understand what exists today and how you can use it today. That means, I don't write very often about healthcare policy or general, public advocacy. My work says "If you are sick or hurt today, and you need help today, here is some information, or some tools, or a way to approach your need for care." It's far more niche than healthcare, but broader than just something like being a smart surgery patient.

If you still aren't sure about your topic and point of view, then try creating a profile of your perfect reader. Male? Female? Or both? What age? Medical problem? Challenge? Where will they live (if it matters.) What kinds of solutions will they be interested in?

Step 2: Based on your topic and point of view, choose a blog name and a domain name.

Your blog's name and your domain name are two different things, although related. Your blog's name can contain your name (or not) or your business name (or not) or even relate to the topic you've chosen. It can be clever, or it can say exactly what the blog is about. Just know that if it's too obscure, it may cost you readers until you are up and running and have established your blogging reputation.

Your domain name is the .com or .ca or .co or .guru or whatever www address someone will use to find your blog. A domain is also called a URL (Uniform Resource Locator.)

- The name may be controlled by the blogging platform you choose, such as myblog.wordpress.com

- Or you may decide to give it its own domain by registering a name that is used only for your blog, such as www.myblog.com

- You may also decide to incorporate it as a section of your website, such as: www.mywebsite.com/myblog. (Your web developer can help you do that.)

Steps 3 and 4 are the actual blog set-up process on the internet. If you dislike the technology parts of working online, then ask someone to help you with these. There **ORB** are links in the ORB to many articles that can help you do this, but if you tend to get frustrated with applications and software, then don't shoot yourself in the foot by insisting you do it yourself. Ask a professional or a savvy friend to work with you.

Step 3: Decide what platform to use for your blog.

The platform is the application you'll use. These are names you've heard like Wordpress, Blogger, Tumblr, or Typepad. Even Google + is considered by some to be a blogging platform. LinkedIn also has a section devoted to blogging. There are dozens of blogging platforms for you to choose from. (ORB)
Most are free. Some charge a nominal amount. **ORB**

One way to make the right choice for you is to decide whether it's OK for your blog to live on the servers of the blog platform you choose, or whether you prefer to host your blog yourself.

When it resides on (is hosted on) the platform's servers, they will give you a name like myblog.wordpress.com or myblog.blogger.com. It will also mean that your blog lives online at their mercy. In the (unlikely) event you violate their policies, or someone complains about your blog, they can take it down. I know this because it happened to me in 2008. Someone had commented on my blog about a psychiatrist in Naples, Florida who was sexually harassing her. She had used his name, he took umbrage, and complained to Wordpress where my blog was hosted. So sure enough, they pulled it offline.[17]

Self-hosting means you have control over your own work, and no one can cause your work to be pulled. More importantly, it means you can use a regular URL like www.myblog.com. But it also means you will pay to have it hosted, most likely at a host that charges you a minimal amount of money to do so (maybe $100 a year), but also keeps it backed up for you plus other services that are useful. In order to use self-hosting you will register your domain, choose a host, apply the blogging software you will use (like Wordpress) then go!

(These resources and links to step-by-step guides are all found in the ORB.) **ORB**

Step 4: Apply your branding to the look and feel of your blog.

Your hosting, whether it is self-hosted or resides on the blogging platform itself, will have themes you can choose from. Themes are the look and feel of your blog – the colors, the logos, whether you have one column or more, and the navigation – the links from page to page.

Every blog platform has dozens or hundreds of themes you can choose from. Each of those themes has dozens of options for look and feel.

The key is to make sure that your blog looks like it belongs to you, that you have branded it well enough to look as if it coordinates, and is in the same family as, your website, your business cards, your brochures – all those graphic representations we know are important.

---

17 http://trishatorrey.com/2008/02/28/when-the-psychiatrist-is-a-bully/

If you are developing a business blog, it is crucial your branding be as close as you can get it to the rest of your materials. If you are developing a more personal expert-focused blog, then you may want your personal branding to reflect your business, but they don't need to be identical. You can put a little personality into your personal, expert blog that may not be an exact representation of your practice.

Examples:
My business website is www.EveryPatientsAdvocate.com
My personal, expertise-focused blog is www.TrishaTorrey.com

You'll see that while they look like they go together, they are different.

Step 5: Start creating!

OK – the set-up is behind you, so it's time to get started with the actually blogging – the content creation.

Your blog will be a representation of you and your expertise, even if your content is focused solely on your business.

I'm a writer. I enjoy writing, I have a voice, and I've done it for years – and a lot! – so writing is how I express myself in my blogs.

But you may choose to make videos. You can upload them to YouTube or Vimeo, and then feature them in your blog too. Still others among you are graphic and image geniuses and can create marvelous poster-looking pieces called infographics that explain concepts or lists or relationships. Still others are happy to chat all day and can create podcasts on many topics to feature on their blogs.

The cleverest among us combine all creative approaches to their content.

I'm not going to tell you what to write or create because your topic and niche are yours. But I can give you some guidelines about content that will serve you well as you begin putting your blog together:

- Be yourself. This isn't about a formal presentation. This is about being authentic; using your own voice, almost as if you are carrying on a conversation. In fact, that takes us to the second guideline...

- Invite interaction. Ask questions or ask for feedback. Getting others to express their opinions means you'll find more people reading your blog because people who comment will share links to your blog to show off where their comments show up.

- Err on the side of too short. Each post does not need to be a master thesis. In fact, if you have a long post, you might consider dividing it into a couple of different posts. (Yes, this is the "do as I say and not as I do" piece of advice.) A good, average post will run 600 words.

- For each text post, include some sort of image that reflects your post. Images attract attention and draw readers even better than videos do because they don't require any time investment to understand them. There are many websites that offer photos, some free, some paid for $1 each on up. See a list in the ORB. (A caveat here: don't add images that you don't have rights to, either by purchasing, or by written permission from the artist or photographer. The internet is full of stories about lawsuits against people who steal images. It's plagiarism. Don't do it.)

- Your headline is important. People love quizzes and lists (50 Ways to Leave Your Lover!) and they particularly love a title that is intriguing, enticing them to delve into the content to see what the mystery is.

- Don't be afraid to be controversial. Now, I'm not saying to intentionally tick other people off. That will just send them away. But I am saying that a little controversy can go a long way toward bringing people to your blog, especially when they don't agree with you. controversy invites comments, and you can then create a point-counterpoint within your comments. Remember, too, that search engines will crawl the comments and their key phrases on your blog, too, so you'll end up with a little unplanned-for google juice by stirring the pot.

- If your post will be mostly a graphic, a video or a podcast, make sure your description in the same post uses the right key words and key phrases so it will be found in search engines. Search engines can "read" only text so anything else you would include needs to be represented by text in some way.

- Vary the content of your posts so your readers won't get bored. I don't mean vary them between written, video, etc, although you may also do that. Instead I mean vary the aspects of the topic you write about. One day you might want to talk about a personal experience, the next day you'll feature a news story and your spin on it, and another day you might review a product you tried. Find some resources in this chapter on page 101 called Blog Fodder.

- Important: don't mix your causes. When it comes to blogging on anything related to your topic, even if it's a bit of a stretch, then go for it. For example, if you are blogging about eldercare issues in Michigan and you find an interesting piece of news about a program in Nebraska, then of course, write about it. The same would be true about a seasonal flu epidemic. Even though the flu isn't only about older people, it would certainly be appropriate.

  But other kinds of topics should be off-limits. Say there are two political candidates running for a state office. You are very upset about one candidate's stance on abortion – but your blog is not the place for that. The minute you take up an issue that is outside your expertise without qualifying it for that expertise, you will begin to lose part of your audience. It waters down your expertise, and may derail it. No one can afford to lose part of their audience!

  If you MUST talk about these two candidates on your blog, you might instead contrast them on eldercare issues, or even senior citizen issues. That fits within your area of expertise, but allows you to support your candidate as well.

Step 5: Collect Email Addresses

One of the most important reasons you'll want to establish a blog is because it's a great place to collect email addresses. When people are interested in your perspective on the topics they, too, find interesting, they will want to opt-in to your further thinking – future blog posts.

Every blog platform has a way to collect email addresses. It might be as simple as having people sign up on the site so that each time you create a new post and hit the PUBLISH button, they will receive an email telling them of your new post. Or, you can add your own email address collector which you will have developed by using an email application (discussed more thoroughly in Chapter Eleven, Newsletters.)

This email collection will be gold. It allows you to reach out to the folks who have opted in as frequently as you would like to, not through your blog, but by any other email-based means.

Believe me when I tell you that blogging need not be any more complicated than what I've outlined here. It is the very best way to be your authentic self, showcase your expertise, interact with others over your own topic, and learn. Just do it!

Blog Fodder

Sometimes we need a little inspiration for blog posts. I can tell you that early in my patient empowerment work (beginning in 2005) it was fairly difficult to find inspiration for my blog. I was new at it, I didn't yet conceive of all the issues involved, and there was little or nothing in the news about problems in the healthcare system. No one was yet talking about healthcare reform, and – a patient advocate? What was that and why would anyone ever need one?

Within two short years, I had just the opposite problem! By 2007 the tide was turning, the presidential elections raised the specter of healthcare reform and patient safety issues had become regular news topics.

These days I can't begin to keep up. There are so very many topics in patient empowerment and patient advocacy. Just the news alone – in any given day there are at least a dozen great national or international articles I would love to highlight for my patient empowerment readers. In fact, my bi-weekly newsletter no longer focuses strictly on my own blog posts because I truly can not stay on top of it all. So now I might highlight one blog post, but then I curate the most useful of the other great articles I've found elsewhere.

All this is what I call blog fodder – resources that inspire (and maybe instigate!) your creative ideas for your blog.

You are already involved in some great resources for your blog. Of course, you can't talk about your clients without their permission (even if you don't mention them by name, they will recognize themselves if you write about them.) But you can write about different problems you've run into with the system, or talk about new things you've learned, or add your two cents to legislation. Maybe you subscribe to a trade magazine, or your local newspaper has a health section. Do you have a favorite saying that applies to your work? A casual question or comment from someone you meet can lead to a great post. Soon you'll find yourself turning every conversation you have into an idea for a blog post.

Write down your ideas as they come to you. Chew on them for awhile. One day the inspiration will come for you to write about them. At any given time I have dozens of ideas for each of my blogs. You will too.

Blog Commenting (On Other People's Blogs)

As mentioned, as you provoke thought through your blog, your readers will comment on your blog. That's a good thing! Even if they don't agree with you, the more people comment, the more they are reading, the more they are sharing, the more google juice you're squeezing, and the more visitors you will have to your blog.

One of our guidelines reminds you that it's OK to be controversial in your posts... and of course, that feeds the commenting public like nothing else.

The one thing you'll want to check in comments is whether they are promoting something, linking to something you don't like or don't believe in. If someone includes a URL in a comment on one of my blog posts, I always check it out. If I don't like it for any reason, I delete it. It's my blog and I have a right to do that – and you do too.

Of particular note on my own blog were many HATE comments during discussion, then passage of the Affordable Care Act. I rarely deleted comments (except for the name-callers and those with too many four-letter words). Their comments were far more a reflection on them than on me, of course. But I would delete any links to any other sites I felt were hateful or wrong-minded. My prerogative!

In reverse, you might want to comment on other people's blogs. A short, pithy, thoughtful comment can go a long way toward getting your name and practice name "out there" – always linking back to your website and your blog, or both. Great promotion.

Just be careful not to be known as a commenting pariah, you know, one of those folks deemed to be obnoxious, who causes others in your topic circles to cringe. That can have only a negative effect on your regard and your business. That includes posting comments that aren't about the blog post but are promotional in nature only.

Guest Posting

Guest Posting is a marvelous two-way street that helps you in a variety of ways.

The first direction is allowing other people to post an entire post (not just a comment) on your blog. You might put together an invitation on your blog that invites them to share their information and opinions – within your own limits. You can see how I have done that here: http://bit.ly/guestpostinvitation   Go ahead – copy me!

The benefits of letting others post to your blog are similar to inviting comments: your posters will send a link to your blog to their friends, or they will post it in social media. Those friends will forward that link to their friends, etc. Plus, search engines love it.

In fact, if you truly admire someone who blogs within your topic area, and you know they have a good following for their own work, you might invite them to publish a guest post at your blog. Some of their followers will check you out if they do.

I will caution you that there is an entire cadre of writers, mostly marketers, who will contact you to inquire about posting a guest blog post that is more about promoting their own website than it is about calling attention to their expertise. These are often law firms (promoting mesothelioma lawsuits or medical malpractice) or sites that list educational opportunities for health-related courses that are built strictly to make money – not to enhance or contribute to your topic area. Caveat emptor contributor. I always say no.

The second direction is for you to write a guest post to contribute to someone else's blog. All the same cautions and rules apply. It will be a great opportunity for them to help promote their expertise, and they will thank you for it. It's win-win. We do this with the APHA website, inviting Premium Members to post guest posts, then link to their own blogs.[18]

Measuring Your Success

Measuring the reach of your blog is very similar to measuring pageviews on your website. Most of the blogging platforms (WordPress, Blogger, Tumblr, etc) will measure pageviews for you, but many of them will also allow you to add the code for Google Analytics.

---

18 Alliance of Professional Health Advocates http://aphablog.com/member-posts

That covers blogging for now, although we could probably go on for pages and pages and pages.

But there's no sense in that. Blogging is a lot like painting your house. Yes, there are guidelines for how to choose the right brushes, or how often to paint your house, or whether or not to take the shutters down before you paint, etc. But the most important aspect is the color you choose and what that says about you as the homeowner....

Included is the fact that if you get started, and you don't like the color, you can always choose a different shade or change the trim....

But remember, just as important as it is to keep your house maintained and painted – and the street numbers on it prominent enough that others can find it – it's important to do the same for your business and your expertise. Blogging is a great tool for that.

Give it a try.

Chapter Ten

Tactic: Social Media

This tactic will:

- Keep you connected with clients, potential clients, influencers and the industry
- Keep you current in your profession and general health information
- Provide a way to be immediately responsive to your marketplace
- Expand your brand across a variety of platforms

If this book had been written in 2008, social media would not have rated its own chapter. I might have made a brief reference to MySpace or even Facebook, and possibly Twitter in a chapter on using the web for marketing. I might have suggested you check out social media to see if you had any interest. Never could any of us have anticipated the growth, breadth, depth, or large impact social media would have on us, in more ways than most of us realize.

Enormous. Powerful. And for advocacy, mostly untapped.

The very fact that it is so enormous makes it difficult to figure out where to begin writing this chapter! Or even which aspects of its use must be included, or which ones to leave out.

So, hoping to provide you with the primer on social media, where it can take you, and how to get started, let's first look at what we mean when we say "social media."

What Is Social Media (or Social Networking)?

I suspect that when asked that question, most of us would simply name a site where social media and networking takes place, like Facebook, Twitter, or even Linked In.

But that's only a part of the story. It's a little like asking, what is transportation? .. and the answer is "a car." In fact, transportation refers to the activity of getting from here to there. A car is just one way to do it, to be transported.

So let's ask again what social media is and this time we'll go broader. Social media is the act of connecting and developing relationships online - networking. Facebook, Twitter, Pinterest and, literally, thousands of other sites are simply tools that help us do so.

For general marketing purposes, social media provides a platform for brands (products, services, businesses) to connect with their customers, clients, influencers, competitors, the media and others they want to reach in an effort to influence them to buy their products or engage their services.

And so it is true for marketing advocacy. Social media can allow you, as an advocate, to connect with your clients, potential clients, influencers, competitors, collaborators, the media –even just the curious in an effort to influence them to engage their services.

What kinds of connecting are we talking about? Any form of communication, like conversations, questions, answers, sharing stories, sharing solutions, empathy and sympathy, laughter, gossip, emotion – you name it. If a human being can communicate it, it can be shared on social media.

One of my favorite descriptions of social media is that it's a 24/7 party, online, requiring only that you show up. It doesn't matter what you wear. You don't have to buy a ticket. And you can talk to, dance with, and develop friendships with anyone you'd like to – even if you don't think you are one of the cool kids.

In fact, participating in social media means you ARE one of the cool kids!

Be One of the Cool Kids – A Solution Provider

Social media's cool kids are simply the people who actively participate on the platform, asking questions, offering answers, and solving problems. So, for example, if you are active on Twitter, and your niche is medical billing, and a question is asked by someone (anyone!) about how to look up CPT codes for free, and you provide the link – you have just become one of the Twitter cool kids – because you participated.

No, there's no list anywhere of who these cool kids are. It's more about the very positive feeling you get because you've participated, helped someone, been appreciated, and will now step into another conversation where maybe you'll help someone else, or maybe someone else will help you.

Here's a real life example:

I joined Twitter in early 2009 and immediately connected with dozens of individuals, including other patient advocates, individuals, doctors and other clinicians. After a few months I was following, and had developed a few hundred followers.

One day I got an email from a woman who was desperate to help her unemployed 31-year-old son who had just been diagnosed with pancreatic cancer. She lived an hour away from him. He had called her because he had no insurance and was being forced to leave the hospital. She was planning to take him back to her house, but the hospital wouldn't give her his records and she didn't know any doctors who would see him. Even if she found one, how could they afford to pay for the doctor's care? She was clearly panicked, and in desperation had reached out to me, a stranger who she found online (through About.com[10]).

Upon receipt of the email, I jumped on to Twitter and asked the question,

> What resources + providers are avail in Ft. Lauderdale
> for a 31yo, unempl man with pancreatic cancer?
>
> (yes – fewer than 140 characters!)

The response was immediate. The question was "retweeted" (shared with other followers) dozens of times. Twenty people, many of whom I didn't follow or didn't follow me, answered with doctor's names, local charitable resources, a national "pancan" organization and more. I compiled the responses into a reply email, and within 20 minutes, had responded to the mom who had written to me.[20]

That made me one of the cool kids on Twitter. A cool kid in my own mind anyway. It drove home the power of social media to solve problems.

Social Media for Marketing Your Business

When marketing is at its best, it is a route to the potential and promise of solutions. That's why we focus on benefits instead of services in our marketing messages – because the potential for solutions, and therefore peace of mind, is what our audiences seek, and sometimes what we also seek for our own challenges.

You can see then why social media can be such a great marketing tool. As business owners, and experts, we would be foolish not to take advantage of those opportunities, to maximize our exposure to those who need our expertise and solutions. Further, it's an excellent learning tool. A shortcut to the input and knowledge we need to best do our jobs.

So how do we get started with social networking? Like other subjects in this book, I could write an entire book for each of the social media platforms and still not completely answer that question. So instead I'm going to get you started, then send you to the ORB for more information.

Which Networks Are the Best for Finding Clients?

Let's begin by figuring out exactly who it is we want to connect with – primary and secondary audiences – and then figure out where (which social media networks) they are spending their time.

---

19 http://patients.about.com For 7 years I wrote articles and a blog on patient empowerment topics at About.com until they ended our contract in 2014.

20 Sadly, about three weeks later, I heard back from the mom that her son had died. She wrote to me to express her gratitude. I just cried.

Note – that does not say we begin by choosing a platform. I'm not going to jump into Facebook, get settled, and then figure out if anyone with an interest in my topic is there. No, I have to decide first if Facebook is the social network of choice for my audiences.

Here's how:

- Start by figuring out who you want to connect with. Who is your perfect client or influencer? Those are questions we answered long ago, so you should just be able to roll those answers off the top of your head.

- Next, what social media are your audiences already using? It should be fairly easy to figure that out. Choose your favorite search engine (Google, Bing, Yahoo) and search using the terms you would use for your own website – and see what networks you come up with.

  For example, if I search using these terms: "breast cancer social media" – then I come up with a Twitter group called the BCSM (Breast Cancer Social Media) Community. I further learn they do a "tweetchat" every Sunday evening. If that's my niche, I need to be there! I also find a breast cancer group on Facebook which may yield other dates or events of note. In any of these situations, you can jump right in and begin to participate. You know – become a cool kid in those two communities.

- But I'll also encourage you to look a little deeper. Facebook and Twitter are bound to be at the top of the SERPs because so many millions of people participate with them. They are enormous ponds, and you will be but a small, new fish. Delving deeper might raise a lesser known social media opportunity, a smaller pond in which you could become a much larger fish in a shorter period of time. So yes, poke around and find another site called www.myBCteam.com which is another social network for women facing breast cancer. There might be some good possibilities there.

- Another great way to search is to use hashtags (see page 114 for a good explanation of where these come from.) Searching #breastcancer actually yields a very different list from a general search like described above.

- The key is to figure out where you can learn the most and give the most in the shortest period of time. That's a good place to get started, although I might test the waters in the larger, more prominently found groups as well.

It may take some trial and error. You may join one network, decide it's not for you, and move on. But you won't know until you try, of course.

Which Networks Are the Best for Networking with Other Professionals?

The other important aspect of social networking is connection with other advocates and industry professionals from whom you can learn so much.

Some social networks are more focused on those connections, promoting business and professional features and applications. They may address personal connections, too, but you'll make more business connections than client connections when you use them.

Of course, let's not forget that those business and professional connections may become influencers, so for that reason, they are also a great bridge to new client connections.

The "Must Do" Social Networks for Advocates

Understanding that some of your social media connections will be oriented toward clients and personal connections, while some may be more focused on business and professional, here are my personal assessments of which networks might be which[21]:

Personal (Friends, Family, Clients)	Business (Network with other professionals)
• Facebook	• LinkedIn[22]
• Pinterest	• Twitter
• Google +	• Google+
• Vine	
• Instagram	

I expect some folks would argue that your friends and family should be kept separate from potential clients – and I would agree. I ran into problems with this one myself. Find the sidebar on page 112 to see what my solution was.

The point to including them on the same list is that individuals' interests, and the conversations you have with them publicly, online, will be very different from those conversations you have with business connections.

There is so much to be said for getting started on each of these platforms. It's also entirely possible that by the time you read this book, there will be a new one that has come along that I haven't even mentioned here!

I've added some network specific information to the ORB, **ORB** like how to get started using them, and some of the insider rules for maximizing your reach on each.

What Are You Supposed to Talk About in Social Media?

Almost anything. But that "almost" does create a few boundaries that can keep you out of social media hot water.

You'll need to draw a line yourself between what is personal, authentic and personality

---

21 You may disagree with my assessment! If you do and you have been successful on another platform, I hope you'll keep doing what you're doing. These lists are to help social media beginners get started and to give them a sense of what is what. But if you have been connecting through social media for a while and it has been working for you, don't stop.

22 LinkedIn is both a resumé showcase and a social media site. Here we refer to its social media possibilities. In Chapter Twelve we'll look closer at its additional possibilities for promoting your expertise.

revealing (all good) from what is too much exposure, too playful, too revealing, and possibly against the law (think HIPAA[23].)

- We've all heard stories of people who have exposed too much on social media and have gotten into trouble. Or, as my daughter describes it, "WTMI – the station of Too Much Information!"

- Yes, there are some things that just should not be shared online, including through social networking. Never expose any client information, or information about anyone at all who would be upset if you shared their personal information. Included would be any information about your business that would give away too much information to a competitor.

- Protect yourself, too, by not giving away too much personal information online. As of publication of this book, I've never heard of an advocate who faced danger from giving away too much information. But we know that it happens to other professionals, like real estate agents, resulting in theft, assault and worse. [24] Don't forget, too, there are security risks from yielding too much financial information.

Those are the negatives – a few caveats:

Now let's look at what content is good to share on social media:

Remember, social media works best to further your goals if you treat it like a conversation, sharing, providing give and take. That's a much better approach than if you simply post things and hope someone reads them. Think of social networking as more like a party and less like a billboard.

Good ideas for social media content:

- Ask questions about any topic relevant to your advocacy. That invites someone to respond, thus creating a connection.

- Promote a new blog post. You don't have to use the actual title. In fact, it might be better to be a bit provocative in your social media post about the content of the blog post.

- Comment or ask a question about a topic in the news with a link to the news story.

- Promote an upcoming public speaking gig.

- Post a tip that relates to your advocacy or your business.

- Link to your latest newsletter. (See Chapter Eleven.) Ask people to opt-in to receive it next time.

- Congratulate someone – for a promotion or a new job, to a new grandchild, to moving into a new home or anything in between.

---

23 HIPAA - Health Insurance Portability and Accountability Act – privacy laws for healthcare.

24 http://bit.ly/redanger

- Post a photo that speaks a thousand words.

- Share a link to a new podcast or video.

- Mention a book you just read and what you learned by reading it (or even what you didn't!)

- Put out a call to "ask an advocate" – then answer the questions people ask.

That's a start. It won't take long for you to identify what you like to post, what gets the best reaction and feedback, and, what sorts of posts are really just a waste of your time.

When to Post and How Much Time to Spend

There is no magic formula for the right time, or the right amount of time to spend on social media.

There are studies that show when the most people are online, friending, tweeting and pinning. (Wednesdays between noon and 1 PM.) But I'm not convinced they are talking about the people we want to reach, like potential clients or other advocates. If our goal is to find THE people we want to rub social network elbows with, I think we need to figure that out on our own.

As we've done several times, think about the people you hope to connect with online. Clients under the age of 65 will likely be online with their social time during a lunch hour or shortly after supper (or after the kids are done with soccer practice.) Over the age of 65? Maybe during the day… but you may have to play with it for a while to figure out some generalizations.

Self-employed business people, like other private advocates, or even doctors or other clinical folks we might connect with could be online with their social media at almost any time. For some platforms you may want to make the effort to catch them in real time (like Twitter). But for others, the actual real time is less important because conversations take place over time (like the Group Forums on LinkedIn.)

As for how much time, there are some guidelines for that. Early in your advocacy practice, before you have a full billable workload, you'll have far more time to test the social media waters. Since you will be marketing your services in this way, it's actually a good way to spend your down time. You may find yourself getting very involved in social networking activities, even a few hours a day. Over time, as your practice matures and more of your hours are devoted to billable clients, you may find you drop in for 10-15 minutes a day just to be sure you have responded to anyone who has DM'd, (direct messaged) or otherwise called for your attention.

Consider setting up regular "chats" on Facebook or Twitter. Set a one-hour time every week on the same day and invite people to ask you questions. OR, set up questions ahead of time and get people to participate. There is information about getting started with chats in the ORB. (ORB)

Your Social Media Persona: Public or Private?

When I first got started on Facebook, it was so much fun! I friended all my family and friends, even hunting down old friends I had lost touch with over the years. I looked forward to updates every day. I posted an update of my own on occasion too. It was all friendly and fun.

Shortly after getting started with Facebook, I set up a second page—for Every Patient's Advocate. That was how I planned to separate my work persona from my family and friend persona.

It didn't work. No matter how I tried to keep them separate, I got hundreds of friend requests from people I didn't really know on my Trisha account, who knew me from my work in patient empowerment. And it put me in a bind. Did I have to inform hundreds of people that they should instead friend Every Patient's Advocate? Talk about a time suck! Or did I just insult them by ignoring them, or not friending them? That's just not me.

Before I even realized what was happening, I had hundreds of "friends" – so many that it was difficult to find the people I really cared to keep up with. It became so frustrating that I stopped using my Trisha Torrey Facebook page all together. And I lost all the fun of it – my friends and family were still posting, they fully expected I was getting the news they were posting, and I wasn't. Then I missed the news when a friend's mother died. I should have been at the funeral and I wasn't – because I didn't know – because I had given up on Facebook.

My solution was to create a new Facebook page using my married name (which is not Torrey.) I still avoid my Trisha Torrey page almost entirely, checking it only 1-2 times a year. Family and friends know I'm there with my married name. I don't accept additional friend requests on my "married" page from anyone except those who are truly inside my inner circle.

And, a bit of Facebook humor, when I tried to say from my new account that I am married to my husband, Facebook informed me that he couldn't be my husband because he is married to Trisha Torrey. So I had to "divorce" him from Trisha Torrey so he could be married to me, whereupon a dozen or more people who are friends of Trisha Torrey all let me know how sorry they were I had gotten divorced.

The bottom line is that you will most definitely want to keep your personas separate if you value your personal privacy. You may have to separate your work personality from your private personality, and make it clear to family and friends which is which – and why.

It's possible with a little creative thinking, no matter who is married to whom.

Social Media Guidelines: Maximizing Your Reach

Just like we had a list of guidelines for effective blogs, there are similar concepts for participation in social media:

- Be yourself. Social media is about people and personalities. Even if you are using it for your business, remember that advocacy is a very people-founded business. People want to know who you are, what you stand for, how considerate or empathetic you are, and more. Be authentically you.

- Remember that all your marketing should refer to all your other marketing. When it comes to developing your profile for each social media choice you make, be sure to include links to your website, your blog and other information that helps people find you when they are ready to discuss their advocacy needs.

- Follow a follower as much as it makes sense. There used to be an unwritten rule in social media that required you to always friend or follow back if someone friended or followed you. But that's an old rule and not only not necessary, but will actually render your social media time almost useless. If you follow too many people, you won't have time to participate with the people you can really learn from, or help. It will be impossible to keep up.

- Don't be too promotional. Remember, social networking is about a conversation, not a billboard. If you are too promotional, people will stop following you. Or worse, you'll think they are following, but they will have muted your posts.

- Be short and to the point: You may remember from *The Health Advocate's Basic Marketing Handbook*, the caveat "the less said, the more read." This is also true with social media. Twitter already forces you to be brief with only 140 characters. You'll have to constrain yourself on the others – but it's worthwhile editing yourself to stay brief.

- Be public with your business posts. I have never understood why someone would take to Twitter, for example, then hide what they have to say. For business purposes, that just does not work. You're shooting yourself in the foot and wasting your time if you insist that your posts be private.

- Participate! Don't be the wallflower at the party! Jump in. Say something. Contribute!

- Now, that's not a carte blanche invitation to talk too much. We all know those folks, and avoid them. Post just often enough. It's possible to post too often, and like with the problem of being too promotional, you'll send followers away if you do. On Twitter you can get away with posting the same thing a number of times during the day (maybe 3-4 hours apart.) Facebook users aren't so generous. Play Goldilocks for yourself and figure out how often is "just right."

- Be a problem solver. Not that you'll always have an answer (nor should you) but you can provide links, connections, introductions and resources when people need them. Everyone else will see how helpful you are – all good for business.

- Always give credit to the person who said something first. Don't ever try to claim someone else's words or concepts as your own. You'll be appreciated for sharing someone else's words but only if you provide attribution.

- Along with giving credit is giving appreciation. Thank others when they share your posts, provide something useful, or say something nice to you.

- Answer questions when they are posed to you. And if you don't know the answer, don't be afraid to say so. If it makes sense you can promise to follow up later with an answer or resource if you think it's worthwhile to do so.

- Don't gossip or share gossip or information from a source that may not be credible. Link to good sources when they are available. We've all learned that news – and gossip – travel fast, and sadly, they somehow become the early truth, even when entirely inaccurate, when they are repeated online. Unless you have found information from a mainstream news source, or a reporter you know to be credible, it's better to just skip a post than it is to repeat wrong information.

- Use hashtags. Begun on Twitter, hashtags have become a way of identifying themes across all social media. A hashtag is not just this -> # - but the words that come after it. So, #patientadvocacy, when popped into a search engine, will yield dozens or more conversations taking place all over social medial about #patientadvocacy.

- Include photos or videos when possible. Graphics and images are always more eye catching and, of course, you want to keep your text brief, but a picture can fill in those thousand words.

- If it makes sense, include your social media "stream" on your website or blog. The comments you make in social media might be just inviting enough to a website or blog visitor that he/she will want to learn more about you. This is easy to set up. Check with your webmaster.

I hope all these do's and don'ts aren't too daunting. They are mostly just common sense, and are very much about the Golden Rule: do unto others in social media the way you hope they'll do for you.

Measuring Your Success

Social media success, like other online efforts, is fairly easy to measure. You need only look to see the size of your list of followers, or friends, plus how often your words are repeated, shared or retweeted or repinned – or whatever your platform calls for.

There are a handful of measurement tools to use with social media that measure your reach. Sometimes they are paired with social media management tools. I've made a list of them in the ORB.

Of course, remember that it's not just about more followers or shares. It's about growing your clientele. You may be highly successful in using social media, but if you don't see an uptick in business, then you may need to focus on some other form of marketing.

Chapter Eleven

Tactic: Email Newsletters

This tactic will:

- Be the most effective marketing tactic for broad promotion of all your activities.

- Allow you to stay in touch on a regular basis with all your audiences.

- Support your brand promises and recognition.

Let me be clear: Direct mail as a marketing tactic is a must for health and patient advocates to include in their marketing arsenals.

There is no more efficient, consistent or inexpensive tactic an advocate can use to put his or her expertise and availability in front of a potential client or influencer on a regular basis.

Direct mail can be postal or "e." It involves sending mail directly to someone who will benefit by receiving it. In the perfect direct mail world, it is sent only to people who have asked specifically to receive your information (called "opting in.")

There are most definitely benefits to direct postal mail (not-so-affectionately called junk mail) that can, at times, trump even direct email. But unless an advocate has many competitors in their marketplace, the cost of development, printing and postage is probably not worth the return. (This makes sense when you think of how many real estate agents use direct postal mail. They do so because they have many competitors in their area.)

The best direct mail solution for private advocates is email newsletters – so that's what I'll cover in this chapter.

Why a Newsletter?

I'm using the term newsletter in this context to describe a piece of email that is more than just a promotional piece. It's not the same as a "blast email" which is a sales term for email that goes out to a large group to promote mostly one thing – items for sale, or a conference or convention, or some sort of announcement.

A newsletter is meatier than that. It will include different types of content. It will be comprised of links to other material, with the newsletter itself containing just enough information to make the receiver want to link to the rest of the story. This will make more sense in the section coming up on what the content of your newsletter should be.

The biggest difference is that a newsletter is intended, and usually received, as having some value in and of itself. Beyond just trying to sell you something (whether that is a product or attendance at a conference), a newsletter is intended to teach the reader something, provide some background information, or showcase something of importance, appealing specifically to his or her interests.

You can see then why it makes sense to focus on an email newsletter in an advocacy environment where we hope to establish recognition for our expertise and capabilities. It's an opportunity to teach our potential clients and influencers about solutions, our environment and our status within it.

The Benefits of Email Newsletters

There are a number of benefits for both your practice and your personal regard as an expert to using email newsletters as a marketing tactic. It is a unique way to make the best of all the other marketing you are doing.

First, direct email can be easily targeted to your audiences. It's not difficult to grow your own lists of email addresses using tactics discussed throughout this book. Just as important, your lists can be segmented according to interests and therefore messaging. You might have one list for potential clients, and another for influencers. Or you might segment them even further, into groups of patients, caregivers, employers, strategic partners and others.

Next, a website or Facebook page or any other web presence you've established is passive; it just waits for someone to visit it. It can't do any outreach itself.

But direct mail is "push" marketing – it's proactive. You push it out to specific people. It shows up where someone's eyeballs already are – in their email inbox. A good headline, right under someone's nose, is eye catching, and as long as the timing is right, creates a call to action that causes someone to react by requesting more information.

Direct email can be responsive in ways other marketing can't be. You can ride the wave of current headlines, make important announcements within minutes or hours, send timely reminders, gain understanding of your audiences from linked surveys, and more. You can't do that with a brochure or a business card, and it's tough to do it with a website. A blog can be quickly responsive, but isn't paired with the "push" too. Thus direct email is your best choice for responsiveness.

The consistency of a regular email contact goes a long way toward building trust. Whether you choose to send a newsletter once or twice a month or even quarterly, people will begin to remember you after two of three of them, and when a possible need arises, they will either go in search of the last one, or they'll eagerly await the next one. You'll remain top-of-mind even if you aren't sitting in their email inbox right at that moment.

The cost of email newsletter outreach is very reasonable when weighed against the possible returns – new business. The biggest cost is your time (unless you can get someone else to do it for you, of course!) But there will also be the cost of the email application you decide to use. (See page 118.)

In general, there is no better way to pull all promotional aspects of your practice and expertise together into one cohesive and effective marketing tool than by development, and consistent deployment, of a direct email newsletter.

The Components of an Email Newsletter

There are five components to an email newsletter:

1. Email addresses of receivers – your audiences.

2. Program / application – needed to manage email addresses, opt-ins, opt-outs and spam.

3. Personality – your branded template, and your attitude.

4. Content – the information you will include in your newsletter.

5. Calendar – timing and frequency of sending it out.

Let's look at them one-by-one.

1. Collecting Email Addresses

This task has been mentioned many times throughout this book, so we'll pull it all together here.

Your goal every day you work (and even some you don't) should be to collect email addresses to use in your marketing. Every email address you collect represents the potential for business, whether it's to hire you for your advocacy expertise, or to invite you to speak in public, or for some other business-related reason. Email addresses are like gold; the currency of business.

The easiest way to collect these email addresses is through your website, blog, social media or other online outreach. Create a page on your site that collects that information – email address and segment, and what their interest is. In Section 2 (below), we'll look at email applications, and setting up your online collection will become clearer.

When you do public speaking, connect on LinkedIn, talk to potential clients or influencers on the phone, stand in line at the supermarket, go to church or synagogue, even if you attend someone else's Tupperware party – anytime you are out and around and have the opportunity to do so, ask for someone's email address.

... with one important caveat....

Be sure they give you permission to send them marketing email like a newsletter. This happens automatically when someone provides an email address through a form on your website. But you need to ask them directly if you collect it in person, or even from a business card.

Getting their express permission is called "opt-in." That means they have agreed that it's OK to send them email that is marketing oriented – they have opted in to your marketing emails. (See the sidebar at right for more about opting in, opting out, and spam.)

That's Step 1 of email collection. Step 2 is to keep track of which audience they are part of. Your largest segment of people will be potential clients, as in patients and caregivers. But you might also collect email addresses of influencers (employers, financial planners, attorneys and others – see Chapter Five). You should also collect email addresses from other professionals like industry people or potential strategic partners.

Maintenance of your lists shouldn't be too difficult. Your email newsletter application will take care of most of the maintenance for you. You probably won't spend any more time on maintaining the email addresses than it takes to add new ones from people who have opted-in, but not online.

2. Using an email program / application

You have heard of these programs, or applications, but you may not have understood what they are or the great services they provide. Constant Contact, iContact, Mail Chimp, aWeber, Mad Mimi, Email Brain – you can get a list in the ORB. (ORB)

They have several functions, and even if it seems like you don't have very many email addresses on your list, they are worth looking into for the type of management they can provide to you. They are all available online and you use them online. They aren't programs you download to your computer.

First, they help you collect and manage your email addresses. Now, if you have collected only a dozen email addresses, this may not seem like a big deal. But believe me, once you

What's the Scoop on Spam?

Short of being everyone's favorite ham-based meat concoction, spam is the "e" version of junk mail. It insults our eyeballs with everything from offers to enlarge body parts we don't have, to informing us about the billions of dollars on their way to our bank accounts from Nigeria.

As a newly minted email newsletter issuer, the LAST judgment you want anyone to pass on your newsletter is that it is spam. And yes, I can guarantee, someone will deem it so.

Spam has become such an intrusion into our lives and email boxes, that many countries have enacted legislation that not only is intended to prevent it, but spells out penalties for the most insistent spammers.[25]

There are some ways to prevent your email from being identified as spam:

1. Use one of the email programs listed in the ORB. They are known by Internet Service Providers and using them means it is less likely your email will be identified, at least by ISPs, as spam.

2. Include an easily found statement right on your newsletter that explains that someone is getting an email from you because they asked for it.[26]

3. Make it very clear on your newsletter that people can opt-out whenever they would like to, then provide the link to make it easy to do so.[26]

4. Accept that some of your email, no matter how carefully you monitor your opt-ins and opt-outs, will be identified as spam, even by people who signed up for it years ago. They have probably changed their minds, so rather than take the time to opt-out, they instead identify it "spam" through their email program (gmail, AOL, Outlook/Live/Hotmail – all allow this practice.) It's frustrating, but very common.

get past 20-25 email addresses, it can be huge. For one thing, when people begin to opt-in and opt-out, you need a way to compare those addresses to your existing list. If someone opts-out, you need a way to keep track so you don't mistakenly add them back (in which case they may report your email as spam.)

Included in the email address management aspect of these programs are forms you can add to your website or blog to help you collect email addresses. You can create those forms easily with the click of a button, and the addition of your own logo. When someone clicks on the form, their information – including whatever fields you have asked them to fill out (e.g. where they live, first name, etc) will go directly into the email address management storage section of the app.

The next thing these apps do is to provide a spam-free environment for sending. You might be surprised to know that most ISPs (Internet service providers like Verizon, Time Warner, Comcast, and others) restrict how much email you can send at one time. So, by sending your email through one of the email apps, you bypass those restrictions. Further, if those ISPs receive a lot of email that comes from one address that hasn't gone through one of the known email apps, they may bounce the email as spam, even if it's just arbitrary. (They honestly do not care whether someone receives your email or not.) The last thing you need is to have your nice newsletter identified as spam! Engaging with an email application is worth it just to prevent that.

---

25 Find links to laws in the ORB.

26 Find a sample here: http://
www.everypatientsadvocate.com/emailnotice

One function to look for as you assess which program you might use, is to be sure that you can download all your email addresses if you decide to move to another email program. You should be able to download not only the ones that are current and deliverable, but also email addresses for people who have opted-out.

Finally, one of the most important functions of these email applications is that they provide you with lots of interesting statistics. Yes – measurement! For each email you send, you will know how many, and who actually clicked on them to open them, which of the links within the email was clicked, how many bounced, and more.

Pricing for use of an email application is usually determined either by the number of emails you send at one time, or within one month. Most of them offer free services for fewer than x email addresses (x might be 100 or 2500!). So check them out.

3. Your newsletter's personality

Can a newsletter have a personality? Of course it can—and should.

Begin by branding it. You'll want to use your logo, the colors that compliment your logo, all those smart branding things we've talked about before. Most of the email apps offer professional templates for your email newsletter. They are often customizable so you can brand them - use the right colors, pop in your logo and your photo, add your content - and you're good to go.

But from there, it needs to reflect you and your own personality. If you are friendly and funny, then let your newsletter contain serious information, but present it in a friendly way. You may choose to share jokes or cartoons - but only if that's your style. Remember - this regular piece of correspondence needs to be authentically you.

4. What content should you include in an email newsletter?

Content is appropriately the most important aspect of sending an email newsletter too. Your content is what will make or break the success of your email newsletter because it's what provides the value.

Let me remind you of your goals:

First - you want to showcase your expertise and all that entails.

Next - you want to provide value, enough so that the newsletter receiver looks forward to opening your email each time it arrives. This supports that feeling of trust - they appreciate the good information you've provided, and feel smarter having read or viewed it.

And - you want to be consistent in all aspects of the newsletter. Consistent quality of content, consistent timing (addressed more thoroughly in a minute), consistent in your branding. Like the value you'll provide, trust is built on consistency too.

You'll also want to think through your real marketing goals. Do you plan to showcase your own expertise? (Is your newsletter intended to promote your expertness?) or is it about your practice and its benefits and services? Or both? If you have a small practice (just you and one or two others) then it's fine to support both.

Also, consider issuing more than one newsletter, one per audience. You'll want one for patients and caregivers, but you might develop a second one for influencers, too – like employers, or union bosses or estate planners or attorneys. Some of the content can be identical, but other parts will be clearly tailored to their audiences.

Once you've decided the marketing focus, everything else should begin to fall into place. The content you provide will all be focused on those goals and audiences. So, for example, if you plan to focus on promoting your own expertise, then you will feature any articles or interviews you have done for the media. If you plan to focus on your practice, you might feature media mentions of your practice. All other content should support those goals and audiences as well.

Even with those goals, creating an email newsletter doesn't have to be daunting. One concern I hear from people considering issuing email newsletters is that they just don't know how they will generate so much information on a regular basis! How can they do that and keep up with their advocacy workloads, too?

To which I answer.... Don't.

You don't have to be the resource for all that content. In fact, unless you are a content producer (blogger, author, broadcaster) anyway, you can make it very easy on yourself by linking to other experts' content. Doing so is win-win-win. The person whose information you feature will appreciate that you've called attention to their excellent work (more pageviews!), your newsletter reader will appreciate that you have "curated" the content (more on this in a minute) and you win because you have quality information to share with your readers, but with a minimum of time investment on your part.

And, too, your newsletter should be manageable to the reader. You don't need to highlight more than 4-5 pieces of content in total (more in a minute) – and even then, no more than 2-3 sentences about each. The goal is for your reader to get a taste for an article or what's on the other end of a link, then click to go to the link. You don't need to provide a synopsis, or rewrite the piece or even review it. Just 2-3 sentences, and click!

So with those goals in mind, let's look at some of the kinds of content you can include in your email newsletter.

First – the MUST INCLUDES. These are the marketing pieces that must be included – otherwise the whole exercise is a giant waste of time.

Whether you are developing a newsletter that is about you and your expertise, or is about your practice and the services you provide (and the benefits to working with you), you must include:

- Your logo

- Your branding, including the right colors, the right typefaces, and any positioning statements (taglines) you have developed for the audience your newsletter is directed to.

- Your name (or someone's name from your organization) – you want it to be personal after all)

- Your web address

- Your phone number

- Your email address

- Call to action – just like on your website – you need to tell people what to do. "Call XYZ Advocates. 555-555-5555 We are here to help you!"

Then you'll add the rest of your articles and other content to fill it out. Keep your audience in mind as you choose what you include:

- If you write a blog, then link to your latest post – or even a post from a while ago that seems appropriate to current events.

- If you, someone from your staff, or your practice has appeared in the media, link to the news or articles where they are found.

- General news about advocacy. This would be included if it helped to support your work, for example, if employers are interested in how other businesses are including advocates in their benefits.

- Local news of interest – either interest tidbits or opinions about problems.

- Health living or patient empowerment tips

- Success stories about clients (de-indentified of course) Ask for permission, change names, but good stories are well-read in newsletters.

- Testimonials – one or two sentence thank-yous with a client's name attached (even if you use only a first name). These don't have to be a focal point of your newsletter, but featuring them off to the side, or at the bottom, can be powerful.

- From there, you can curate everything else. I actually keep a file on my computer desktop where I keep track of articles, blogs, videos, books and anything else I think my readers will be interested in. I put them in newsletters by writing out the headline, the resource, and a few sentences about why I think they'll be interested.

  Example:

  15 diseases doctors often get wrong
  (which is linked to: http://www.cnn.com/2014/08/26/health/diseases-doctors-get-wrong/index.html)

  Have you been diagnosed with any of these diseases? Or, do you have these symptoms but you can't get diagnosed? See which ones doctors struggle with so you can talk to your doctor about them. (From CNN)

Where do you find all this good information? From a variety of resources. I find most of the articles I curate linked from Twitter. You can find them online at news and mainstream magazine sites, at LinkedIn or Facebook. Someone might send you a link (people who receive your newsletter might begin sending you these because they "know you'll want to share it with others"). You might find an interesting article linked from someone else's newsletter – I often do. You can even include appropriate jokes and riddles.

Finally, like in your blog, don't be afraid to spark a little controversy! The best thing that can happen is for one of your newsletter receivers to respond, even if it's only to argue with you. Those folks are often the most loyal of clients, eventually, because you've been willing to discuss difficult subjects with them.

5. The Calendar – timing and frequency

How often do you need to send your newsletter? The answer will be a function of how much material you have to share, how much people actually do contact you when they have received one, and how much of your marketing time you are willing to devote to it.

My best advice is to start somewhere, stay consistent for a few issues, then adjust. So, for example, you might begin by sending one newsletter a month, but you find when you get better at it, that you can send two each month. If you have a larger practice (more than 2-3 advocates), a good-sized email list (>200 email addresses) and plenty of curated material, then go ahead and step it up to once each week.

You might also consider issuing newsletters to your different audiences on differing schedules. Maybe you send one to your potential clients twice a month, but to your influences only once a month.

Whatever frequency you choose, stay consistent. If you decide to send them less frequently, then warn people in the prior email so they won't be expecting your newsletter, and find they are disappointed (loss of trust!) when they don't receive one.

Some Additional Email Newsletter Guidelines

Here is some additional general advice to help you get your email newsletter started – and growing:

- Attribution: Credit where credit is due! Always be sure that you provide attribution for every piece you publish. In the example of an entry on page xx, you'll see that I said 'From CNN" before the title of the article. You don't have to do it exactly that way, but always be clear. "I read the following post from my friend Georgie Porgie this week, and thought I would share it with you." Or "From the Wall Street Journal's Empowered Patient column, April 2015" – or create your own style. This shows strength in the breadth of sources and in your regard for other professionals.

- Simplicity: If you have to err on one side-er-tuther (as Gramma used to say) then keep your newsletter simple. Don't overwhelm your readers, and don't try to out-fancy the basic template. Simple and clean yields more impact.

- Still not sure? Or looking for new ideas? Subscribe to other email newsletters that might parallel what you hope to accomplish. Look for other professionals in similar industries – like health coaches or geriatric care managers, and sign up to receive their newsletters. Then watch their process. What do you like? What don't you like? Then apply what you've learned to issuing your own newsletter. (If you're looking for an easy one to review, sign up for my personal newsletter at: http://everypatientsadvocate.com/opt-in)

Measuring Your Newsletter Success

Like other web-related marketing, measurement is quite easy for email newsletters. The email program you choose to use will provide you with most of what you'll want to know. You can experiment by including links to more or fewer articles.

Of course, the most important measurement is your new favorite question when your phone rings, "How did you hear about us?" In this case, I recommend you delve a little further by asking "Do you receive our newsletter?" If the answer is yes, then you know it supported the idea of phoning you. If they do not, well then, what are you waiting for? Add them to your list.

Chapter Twelve

Tactic: Miscellaneous Web Marketing Opportunities

Seems like we've gone on and on with opportunities for online marketing and promotion, doesn't it?

And yet, we still have another web marketing mile or two to go.

We've covered the next steps in what to include with your website. Then we looked at the importance of blogging, especially if you are hoping to establish your expertise, and may wish someday to do paid speaking. Social media was our next big step in online promotion. And then the big marketing daddy – newsletters, which can feature the highlights of everything you do.

This last chapter is a gallimaufry[27] of promotional possibilities for the web.

What they all have in common is that they help us do some of the basics that are good for all your web presence(s):

- They showcase capabilities both for you and your practice.

- They allow you to connect with others even though they aren't really considered to be social media.

- They keep you informed of what is going on in your world; not just advocacy, but whatever your topic or subject is as a niche, also.

- They allow us to continue building our authority because we make sure that all our online presences link to the others, providing us with a little extra google juice each time.

---

27 Gallimaufry: my new favorite word. In fact, I now have a section on my personal website called Gallimaufry. It means hodgepodge, mélange or potluck.

Article Writing

Writing for the web is very different from other forms of writing, like magazine articles, letters, books or others. Blogging is great practice, but is usually either opinion or advice. Online articles are usually fact-based.

Writing articles ("online content") can be a great way to showcase your expertise and advocacy practice. You can write articles to post on your own website or blog, and search engines will pick them up, directing people to your website or blog.

Beyond your own web properties, there are dozens of websites that look for good articles, some of which pay their writers. Called "content aggregators," they seek a variety of types of articles, from lists, to how-to articles, to interviews, case-studies, product reviews, white papers and others. They usually feature dozens, or hundreds of topics. You'll recognize their names: Huffington Post, About.com, Ask.com, WikiHow, Answers.com, Examiner, Next Avenue, and others.

Or, if you are a good enough writer, you may be invited to write for one of these websites. You'll need to reach out to them to ask about how they work with writers, and they'll expect you to either "pitch" ideas, or they will ask for samples of your writing. The best ones will pay handsomely for your work.

Lately some new types of information-promoting websites have begun to reach out to writers on specific topics to get them to write articles, answer questions, or otherwise develop content that will live at that one site. They don't pay for the content. Instead the 'trade' for a link back to the author's website or blog. An example of this type of site is NerdWallet.com which a number of advocates have written articles to answer questions about medical billing and claims.

A couple of caveats about article writing at other websites:

As an advocate, your core business (source of revenue) is not writing. You need to weigh the amount of time it takes you to write for these sites against the time you won't have to market (probably more effectively) in other ways. For example, writing for a national website won't help you much if your clients are all in Springfield. Writing, when done well and correctly in a way you want to represent you, is time consuming and may not be worth the effort you expend.

But remember, too, that if you publish articles on someone else's website, to read any contract you may sign very carefully. A phenomenon called "digital sharecropping[28]" means that once someone else publishes your work, they, in effect, own it, even if contractually they tell you they don't. They may tell you that you will maintain the rights to your own material, but that they have the right to use your material, too. Or they may tell you that by paying you, they are purchasing the rights. Or they could ask you to promise that as long

---

28 http://www.copyblogger.com/digital-sharecropping/

as they use your material (whether or not they have paid you), you cannot use it yourself, but once they no longer use it, the rights revert to you. Or any variation thereof.

I write all this to you having suffered the results of the loss of my "crop" of writing at About.com after seven years and thousands of blog posts and articles. Yes, I learned about the losses from digital sharecropping the hard way.

Article writing for online publication can be a great boon to your marketing. Just be sure you understand the time commitment, details, pros and cons before you give it all away and don't get what you need, or are promised in return.

Publish a Book or an E-Book

Beyond writing articles, you might also consider writing a book, or a booklet, that you can publish online.

These days you don't have to wait for a publisher to decide your idea is all-that. You can self-publish quite easily, making you the "author of" – a distinguished position, a very nice addition to your resumé, and a rank higher in your expertise and expertness.

Choose a topic you can exhaust in a few short chapters, or a list of things people should know. Maybe elaborate on your favorite topic from your public speaking. Ask yourself: what do my clients and potential clients wish they knew? What will pique their curiosity?

Then you have your choice. You can put a price on your book, and sell it online. But here's the real bonus of writing a book or an e-book. That is, you can get it printed (digitally, on-demand) and it becomes a great giveaway for new clients, the times you do your public speaking, or in trade for someone's email address (see Chapter Seven.) Everyone loves something for free!

The best combination is to put a price on the cover as if it is available for sale, but then give it to people for free. That way they consider that it has real value – far more than a freebie would have. They will be even more willing to trade a "mere" email address for it.

Those are great dividends: being the "author of" and easy gathering of email addresses. Believe me, it's worth the trouble to publish a booklet.

If you have interest in publishing a book, either in print or "e", find resources in the ORB.

(ORB)

Using Multi-Media

Sometimes YouTube, Vimeo, Blog Talk Radio, SlideShare, and other audio and video type applications get lumped in with social media. But I don't really see them that way. I think of them as tools.

If you enjoy appearing on camera, or like to work in broadcast media like creating podcasts or Powerpoint slides, and can provide tips, or commentary, interviews, how-tos or any other form of interesting audio or video presentation, then using these tools might be a good marketing move.

In fact, one of the best uses for video is to assure a potential client that you are smart, knowledgeable and caring by creating a video for your website or blog. When they see your face, hear your voice, and observe your body language in a video, they will realize how authentic and compassionate you are. That's when they will dial the phone, already sold that they will be in good hands—yours.

It's not difficult to create a video. Begin by scripting what you want to say—not word for word, but concepts like some of the benefits of working with you, and the empathy you want to share—no more than one or two minute's worth. Practice in front of a mirror. Don't be stiff or formal—just be you! Then ask someone with a high-end smartphone or regular video camera to record you, or use the camera built into your laptop. You don't need high-end production values. You just need to reveal the inner compassionate and authentic you. Once you're happy with your video, upload it to YouTube or Vimeo, then ask your webmaster to drop it into your website or blog. (Find more video tips in the ORB.)

One last key to maximizing the use of multi-media. That is, don't let them just stand **ORB** alone. Remember, search engines can read only text—not images, sound or video. So be sure to caption them well using your keywords and phrases – enough to give them plenty of google juice.

Email Signatures

I know. You think this is a stretch calling your email signature a form of online marketing. But hear me out.

Especially when you exchange email with someone new, there's no easier (or less expensive) way for them to be impressed by you than by seeing a list of your accomplishments and showcases in your email signature.

Now, I'm not suggesting you list everything you have ever accomplished of note in your signature!

What I am suggesting is that you set up a variety of signatures, and pull out the right one for the right person at the right time.

For example, I have one signature I use for routine APHA business. I have another one I use the first time I respond to a patient who contacts me through Every Patient's Advocate with a question. I have still another one I use when I pitch articles to magazines and online content aggregators. Some are longer or shorter than others. In total I have 9 different signatures.

What I don't do is include a logo in my signature. You might want to include one – they do look terrific when someone opens your email. But I also know that a graphic image can be a trigger that suggests to your receiver's email program that your email might be spam. I send email to so many different people I don't know, and who don't know me, that I just prefer not to include that extra suggestion that my email looks like it might be spam.

Online Resumés

It seems that most of the places we have a presence online represents just a piece of us. Your Facebook page may be representative more of your personal life than your work life. Your website might represent your work, but only one part of it. Your Twitter or Pinterest or YouTube are usually related to one interest or topic....

Where can you pull all of you and links to your various web presences together into one place? If someone wants to know who YOU are – all the pieces and parts of you – where can you put it, and where can they go?

LinkedIn is the master resumé site, of course. LinkedIn is many things (including social media) but at its core, it's the place you describe your career and all its elements. It's a chronology that answers the "how and why did you become a patient advocate?" question. For those of us who are transitioning and building second and third careers, it gives the backstory. Whether you are employed by someone else, or doing your own thing, LinkedIn provides a place to showcase those elements you want to showcase.

There is a second website where you can provide an overview that is much more graphically appealing, and lots more "at a glance." It's called About.me. It allows some photos and some bullet points. It's sort of "me at a glance" rather than the in-depth description you can add to LinkedIn.

Both LinkedIn and About.me allow you to create more authority by linking to your business and personal websites. Either one can be used in place of many other links in your email signature as well. One clean citation through a link to LinkedIn or About.me can be very clean and professional looking in one email signature.

Web Advertising

Just like advertising on TV, radio, or in print, there are web ads, too. You've seen them everywhere, no doubt. And you may wonder whether they would work for you.

I don't have an answer for you. What I can do is provide some basics, then some resources so you can decide whether it's of interest to you.

The key, like for all advertising, is to make sure your ad is seen by the people who need an advocate. There may be websites you know of that are go-to online locations for the people who might need you, but just like running any other kind of ad, they are difficult to target unless your niche is so specific that you know your potential clients go to them.

For example, if you work only with ALS patients, then a website for ALS caregivers might be a perfect place to run an ad. Or if you have a good team in place for negotiating medical bills in Springfield, you might run an ad in the Health section of the Springfield online newspaper.

If you can be that specific about your audiences, then contact those websites and ask how much it costs to run an ad on their site. The instructions for figuring out whether the cost is worth it to you can be found in Chapter Nine of *The Health Advocate's Basic Marketing Handbook* .

Most of the ads you see online come from an advertising aggregator which places your ads in the 'right' places. You then pay by the number of clicks on your ad. That seems like a good deal, right? You only pay if someone chooses to look at your link? But looking at your link doesn't necessarily translate to business. It might be curiosity, it might be a kid messing around, it might even be a competitor trying to cost you money.

The "right" places are based on key words and key phrases. You might choose key words like "patient advocate Chicago", so that every time someone uses those words in a search, your ad will show up, right there, ready for someone to click on it. The amount you pay for PPC ("pay per click") advertising varies according to the words you have chosen. You might pay 50 cents per click, or you might pay $15 – more or less.

Its cost and results vary so much that it's impossible to make a recommendation for or against web advertising.

Find links to more information about web advertising in the ORB. (ORB)

Online Support Groups

In-person support groups can be found in many places, from churches to community centers, synagogues and schools. You can often find health-related support groups in hospitals and large doctor practices too. Why? Because for those hospitals and practices, they are great marketing. They keep people coming back because they find some relief for their FUDGE.[29]

And yes, if attending support groups is your "thing" then I say go for it if you have something in common with the attendees. If you don't have whatever that "something" is in common with them, then you risk being considered an untrusted outsider. Don't bother.

In this day and age, for a variety of reasons, many people go online to find support. Those reasons include convenience, a wish for privacy, an inability to easily get out to a local

---

29 FUDGE = Fear, Uncertainty, Doubt, Guilt and Exhaustion. Learn more in *The Health Advocate's Basic Marketing Handbook.*

support group meeting, or even that they suffer from a disease or condition that is so rare that finding a local, in-person support group just isn't possible.

As in any support group, there may be people of many ages and cultures and both genders in health-related support groups. There will also be people who have recently been diagnosed, others who have lived with their illness or condition for a long while. Still others may be caregivers, but not suffer from the malady under discussion themselves. Some may not even be diagnosed yet, but are trying to assess symptoms before they even see a doctor.

Sometimes there are professionals who take part in these groups too. You can be one of those professionals.

There are several reasons why participating in online support groups can be useful to you; marketing is really only one of the reasons. The most important reason is because you can "listen" (by reading) and learn.

Your key to entry will be whatever it is you have in common with the group. For example:

- A group for caregivers of elderly parents
- A group of parents for children with cancer
- A group for people who share a rare disease, including their caregivers
- A group for people who can't get diagnosed
- And many others.

The key to participation in any support group is trust. You must build trust. You do that by being respectful of the people who are already there, by not chiming in unless you have something significantly useful to say, and by keeping your mouth shut (your fingers still!) when it comes to anything gossipy. Most online support groups have rules – written and unwritten – so it's important to listen and learn long enough to figure those rules out.

Every support group, whether it's in person or online, has its own personality and its leaders. Sometimes there is a monitor or moderator (the "mod") who keeps the rabble-rousers, rule breakers and rude people in check.

Some support groups allow you to develop an associated profile that tells who you are and what your interest is. Sometimes members prefer to stay anonymous – a fair privacy step. But remember that when they are anonymous that also means you may be getting half a story, a half-truth, an exaggerated answer....

If you want to participate in a support group for marketing purposes, then be sure your connection to the group is clear (your current or previous experience that makes you one of them). I also suggest you be very transparent in your profile that you are a patient advocate, and be sure someone who finds your information can connect with you if they would like to. You can also create a signature for each of your posts that includes something that mentions your advocacy.

Other than that, I would lay low on mentioning that you are an advocate. Instead, ask lots of questions, provide resources if possible, tell stories – just be very helpful. But don't blatantly offer to work for someone, or be too obvious about business purposes for participating. It can be considered obnoxious and could get you bounced from the group.

If this is a new arena for you, and you'd like to find support groups that could work for you, I've provided a list of possibilities in the ORB. ORB

Online Forums and Discussion Groups

Not unlike online support groups which usually focus on people who share health-related challenges, you may find online forums or discussion groups which will be profession or interest related.

These are discussions that take place over time. Someone might post a question, or a statement, or a link to an interesting article. Then he or she will wait while others who are part of the group post answers, or advice, or additional questions or links. This may take place over the course of a day, or even weeks, until that conversation is exhausted and others take its place.

There are several advocacy-related discussion groups, most taking place through LinkedIn Groups.

Included is my favorite (and yes, of course, I'm biased) - the Alliance of Professional Health Advocates Discussion Forum. Adjunct to our Alliance Forum are Special Interest Group Forums including medical billing, Canadian members, lawyers, physicians and some regional conversations too.

If you are a member of APHA but aren't yet participating in the Forums you can't imagine what you are missing.

And of course, I've added more information about discussion groups and forums to the ORB.

ORB

Conclusion

Go Forth and Market to Success

By the time you've read through both marketing books, implemented the various strategies and tactics outlined in them, decided which ones do, and don't, work for you, and you have tweaked them just SO, to make them work even better, well, then....

You will be a more knowledgeable advocacy marketer than I am. Or at least, you will have weathered many more attempts.

I dare say, too, that you will know more about applied marketing than some college professors teaching today who understand psychology, business and theory, but have little practical application experience.

The ORB!

Resources and references change so frequently that I've decided to include them, with live links, online. To that end, I have built

The ORB – the Advocate's Online Resource Bank.

You'll see this logo ORB which shows you that resources for that section have been added to the site at:

www.HealthAdvocateResources.com/ORB

You'll find references to the ORB throughout the book. It will stay updated with new resources, or updates to the links for current resources. This will serve you far better than making you type out all those long web addresses.

Six Months from Now

As mentioned in Chapter One (SWOT Analysis), you should plan to review your marketing every six months or more often to be sure you are on track. That is what will give you the best sense of what is – or is not – working for you, and plenty of time to make adjustments before you spend too much time or money on a strategy or tactic that needs to be reconsidered.

At any time, I invite you to provide feedback about the material I've provided in these marketing books. I'd love to hear about your experiences, in particular what works best. No tactics will be entirely dismissible because everyone's practice is different. But some will work better across a wide spectrum of practices.

Currently there are no more general marketing books in my plans. I do anticipate writing a few more niche-type booklets but have not assigned any completion dates for them yet. If you think of a topic you wish I would cover, please just let me know. My email box is always open: trisha@epadvocate.com

. . . .

I wish you good marketing thoughts going forward. I surely want to see you succeed!

I shared this quote from the Indian Chief Seneca in the Basic book, but it is just as appropriate for this book, too:

> *Luck is the point at which preparation meets opportunity.*

You are now well prepared for every opportunity you seek, and for those which find you as well.

About the Author

When Trisha Torrey was diagnosed with a rare, aggressive lymphoma in 2004, she was a marketing consultant who knew almost nothing about healthcare. She was also naïve to the dysfunction of the American healthcare system that was tasked with treating her.

But she got smart, fast. She learned that the possibility of excellent care was too easily and frequently eclipsed by miscommunication and mistakes. She also learned that if she didn't stick up for herself, and insist on the help she needed, she would not get it. The more empowered she became, the more she realized there was a possibility she had no lymphoma. Eventually she proved she was right; she had no cancer.

Once Trisha put that "no cancer" odyssey behind her, she decided it was up to her to apply her skills to teaching others how to navigate the dangerous landscape of American healthcare. She sold her marketing company in 2006 to devote herself full time to the cause.

Today Trisha calls herself "Every Patient's Advocate." She is the founder of AdvoConnection.com and the Alliance of Professional Health Advocates which support the business aspects of a health advocate's work. She speaks to groups of patients and professionals, and teaches workshops. She is the author of four books: *You Bet Your Life! The 10 Mistakes Every Patient Makes (How to Fix Them to Get the Health Care You Deserve), The Health Advocate's Start and Grow Your Own Practice Handbook, The Health Advocate's Basic Marketing Handbook* , and this book, *The Health Advocate's Advanced Marketing Handbook.*

Trisha has been quoted by CNN, the Wall Street Journal, O Magazine, U.S. News and World Report, NPR, Scientific American, Angie's List Magazine, Bottom Line Publications, and others.

She lives in Central New York State with her husband, Butch, and her mini-mutt, Crosby. When she's not doing her patient advocacy thing, she enjoys playing golf, travel, gardening, and working in stained glass.

Twitter: @TrishaTorrey
LinkedIn: www.LinkedIn.com/TrishaTorrey
Google+:   http://gplus.to/trishatorrey

Index

Index (continued)

The Health Advocacy Career Series

Find all these books linked from:
http://HealthAdvocateResources.com

1. **So You Want to Be a Patient Advocate?**
   Choosing a Career in Health or Patient Advocacy
   Do you have the knowledge and experience to either get a job or start your own practice? How much money can you make? What is the Allegiance Factor and how can it affect your work and your job satisfaction?

2. **The Health Advocate's Start and Grow Your Own Practice Handbook** People like you, with heart and great advocacy skills, want to choose private advocacy as a career, but too often lack the business skills needed to start and grow an independent practice. Includes all the basics, like developing financials, understanding legal and insurance, setting your prices, contracts, forms, best practices and more.

3. **The Health Advocate's Basic Marketing Handbook**
   Makes marketing your advocacy services far easier than you might imagine. Includes all the basics: planning, target audiences, messaging, branding, advertising, public relations, branding and more.

4. **The Health Advocate's Advanced Marketing Handbook** (The book you are reading now.)

5. **The Health Advocate's Low and No Cost Marketing Ideas Handbook**
   Contents as titled. To be published late 2015.

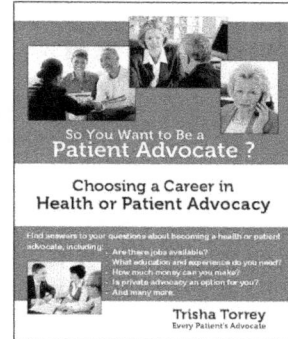

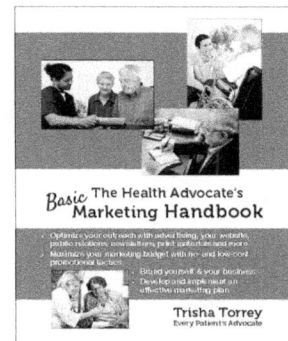

To be published in late 2015:

The Health Advocate's Low & No Cost Marketing Ideas Handbook

General Information

Much more information about the business of advocacy and marketing for advocates can be found in these resources:

www.HealthAdvocateResources.com

Organization:
The Alliance of Professional Health Advocates
for advocates in private practice and those who wish to explore advocacy career possibilities.

ADVC-Connection DIRECTORY
Patients and caregivers find advocates to help them in the **AdvoConnection Directory**

APHA Business & Marketing Workshops
These workshops are held throughout the year in cities across the US. They are focused on business and marketing for private, professional advocacy practices.

The APHA Blog
showcases current thinking, business tips, useful resources and more.

The Health Advocate's Code of Conduct & Professional Standards

Subscribe to let potential clients know of your ethical health advocacy business practices.

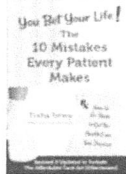

You Bet Your Life!
can teach you how the healthcare system works, and how to work around the problems to get what you - or your clients - need.

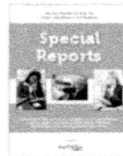

Special Reports...
are available only for short periods of time.

No special reports currently available.

Anyone with interest in Patient Empowerment or Patient Advocacy is invited to join our **Google+ Patient Empowerment and Advocacy Community.**

www.ingramcontent.com/pod-product-compliance
Lightning Source LLC
Chambersburg PA
CBHW081542220326
41598CB00036B/6535